The God-Powered Life

The

God-Powered

LIFE

Awakening to Your Divine Purpose

Rabbi David Aaron

TRUMPETER

Boston & London · 2009

TRUMPETER BOOKS
An imprint of Shambhala Publications, Inc.
Horticultural Hall
300 Massachusetts Avenue
Boston, Massachusetts 02115
www.shambhala.com

9 8 7 6 5 4 3 2 1

First Edition
Printed in the Canada

♾This edition is printed on acid-free paper that meets the American
National Standards Institute z39.48 Standard.
♻This book was printed on 100% postconsumer recycled paper. For
more information please visit www.shambhala.com.

Distributed in the United States by Random House, Inc.,
and in Canada by Random House of Canada Ltd

Library of Congress Cataloging-in-Publication Data
Aaron, David, 1957–
The God-powered life: awakening to your divine purpose/
David Aaron.—1st ed.
p.   cm.
Includes bibliographical references.
ISBN 978-1-59030-652-9 (pbk.: alk. paper)
1. God (Judaism). 2. Spiritual life—Judaism. 3. Self-actualization
(Psychology)—Religious aspects—Judaism. 4. Joy—Religious
aspects—Judaism. I. Title.
BM610.A246 2009
296.7—dc22
2009024347

Contents

In loving memory of my dear parents
Moshe Yosef ben David Leib and Golda z'l
Liba bat Shlomo and Hodel z'l

I am forever grateful for your unconditional love.

Acknowledgments

GREAT THANKS to my wife, Chana. Her unconditional love has inspired and empowered me to discover and feel God's love. This book was made possible because of her consistent support to learn, grow, and teach.

Many, many thanks to my talented editor, Elicia Mendlowitz, who did an exceptional job helping me put this wisdom to writing. I am also thankful to Uriela Sagiv for adding her professional touch, giving these ideas even greater clarity.

My heartfelt appreciation to Beth Frankl of Trumpeter Books for her expertise, advice, and relentless encouragement to seek excellence.

I am extremely grateful to the many friends and supporters of Isralight International, whose generosity has provided me with the opportunity to present the ideas of this book. Special thanks to Robby and Helene Rothenberg, George and Pam Rohr, Andrew and Shannon Penson, Sean and Lindy Melnick, Dr. Michael and Jackie Abels, Dr. Herb and Irena Caskey, Leonard and Dorothy Sank, Nancy Beren and Larry Jefferson, Alexander Beren Jefferson, Dr. Bob and Sarah Friedman, Moshe and Sarah Hermelin, Aba and Pamela Claman, Steven Alevy, Robyn Barsky, Steve Eisenberg, and Tzvi Fishman for their consistent love and support.

I am also grateful to the many students who have attended my talks, Isralight seminars, and retreats. Your questions, challenges, and receptivity have enabled me to access and share these sacred teachings.

I am forever in debt to my holy teachers, especially Rabbi Shlomo Fischer *Shlita,* for all their brilliance and warmth.

Thank you, God. Serving your purpose fills and thrills me.

DAVID AARON
JERUSALEM

Introduction

Sometimes I come home at night and feel really hungry. So I open the fridge, but nothing in there speaks to me. Certainly not the leftover tuna casserole, and not the ready-in-minutes soy burger, not even the home-made stuffed cabbage. I go through what's in there, but everything lacks appeal. So I close the fridge door. And then I come back a couple of minutes later, and I open it again. And it's the same story; nothing has changed in the last couple of minutes. So I close the door, and I walk away, but I am still hungry, so I try again, as if in the last few minutes some little elves had put a treat in there for me.

We have all had the experience of opening and closing the door to the refrigerator, which might be full, but for some reason holds nothing that might satisfy our hunger. That's because what we're looking for is not in the refrigerator—it's in the freezer. Just kidding.

The truth is, what we're looking for is not even food. The soul feels hungry, and we confuse the soul's hunger with a hunger for food and hope that we can satisfy it. And of course we can't, though often we try. Sometimes we think we can satisfy that hunger with food, sometimes with new clothing, a new car, new electronic gadgets, or whatever. We hope that somehow the emptiness that we feel inside can be filled with things, but that never seems to work.

Occasionally, we manage to achieve a temporary respite, a temporary lift, but then that gnawing emptiness returns. And we don't know what to do.

This book is about understanding why we feel that way and learning how to respond to it. It is about satisfying that profound hunger by tapping into our deepest resource for personal fulfillment and genuine self-worth.

You may be shocked when you realize how full you already are—from within. Most of our problems are rooted in our narrow perceptions of ourselves and our lives. We are selling ourselves short and ripping ourselves off. Indeed we are all infinitely greater than we think we are, and our lives are intrinsically more meaningful. The way to connect to and fully appreciate this fact is by discovering our eternal and internal connection with the Great I—God.

Feeling and expressing this divine connection is the most vital work we can do in our lives because only through our connection with God—who is the source of our ultimate self-worth—can we become the best we can be, and only then can we truly feel fulfilled, happy, and at peace with ourselves and others.

To live our connection with God, we have to first understand who we really are. According to the Kabbalah, the mystical understanding of the Torah, each and every one of us is no less than an individualized expression of God—the Great I and Ultimate Self. The more we live up to who we already are in essence, the more we connect with God's endless wisdom, creativity, love, power, and goodness and serve as a unique channel for the Divine Presence on Earth. This is the secret to personal fulfillment and self-actualization (chapter 1).

To accomplish this we must be free to transcend our ego (chapter 2), courageously face our existential loneliness (chapter 3), and integrate the conflicting drives of the two sides of our self—the sacred and the creative (chapter 4). We then experience extraordinary divine self-worth—unconditional self-worth—and our lives become a profound synergy of creativity and stability. We are filled with dignity, having achieved mastery over our environment, and we experience spiritual completeness, having achieved mastery over our inner self (chapter 5).

Precisely at the ecstatic height of enjoying unconditional self-worth we must, however, diligently take care to remind ourselves that the awesome grandeur we sense within us is not *our* grandeur but God's. Otherwise, our egos use these powerful feelings of high self-esteem to alienate us from our true self rooted in God and accessed only by living our divine purpose.

But what is our divine purpose? The Kabbalah teaches that although God is already good and whole, there is an aspect of God that freely wants to justifiably achieve goodness and wholeness through struggle, choice, and hard work. We are that aspect of God. All our flaws, weaknesses, and problems are absolutely essential to fulfilling our divine destiny. Our divine purpose on Earth is to overcome the bad and boldly choose to become good, whole, and godly (chapter 6).

Serving God's purpose brings us serenity, inner peace, and happiness. Every fleeting moment is infused with eternal meaning whenever we choose goodness over evil, love over hatred, truth over falsehood, trust over despair; we fulfill our divine purpose in the here and now (chapter 7). Everyday life becomes full and momentous when we learn how to lovingly serve here and now. Happiness is always a matter of choice when we see in every challenge an opportunity to serve and grow toward our greater goodness, wholeness and godliness (chapter 8).

God asks us to be holy: "You shall be holy, because I, your God, am holy."[1] Holiness means feeling wholeness, being whole with who I am, whole with what I am doing, whole with the moment I am doing it in, whole with whom I am doing it for, whole with doing it for the one who is absolutely whole—God. When we choose love and do good deeds because of their intrinsic value and not because we want some future benefit in return, then every fiber of our being is alive here and now and filled with God's presence. The Kabbalah offers us a clear road map directing us in how to become whole; how to align our individual self with the Universal Self and serve to channel God's presence into everything we think, say, and do (chapter 9).

In the final analysis, however, healthy and happy souls remain forever lovesick for God because the more conscious we are of our soul's desire to live our divine purpose and connect with the Great I, the more sadness we feel over the lack of greater connection. Paradoxically, happiness lies precisely in the depth of this sadness. It propels us forward in our spiritual journey, invigorating and motivating us. It guarantees that the journey and adventure of love, goodness, and wholeness will never end. And on our endless journey there is endless joy in our anticipation of getting forever closer and closer to our Divine Endless Self (chapter 10).

I sincerely hope that the ancient teachings presented in this book will inspire and empower you to live a life of transformation, fulfillment, and unconditional self-worth—here and now. Remember, life is not a race but a journey. And God is with you every step of the way.

A note about conventions: The Great I—the one who is the Creator of the world, who is both transcendent and yet immanent—has many names (some of which are mentioned in this book), but it seems impossible to write a book in the English language without accepting conventions and using the word "God." Also it seems impossible to avoid the pronoun "he" without resorting to convolutions of English usage. The Endless One manifests sometimes in masculine ways and sometimes feminine ways and is indeed beyond all anthropomorphic constructions. However, I have reluctantly acceded to using the pronoun he, even though it can be very misleading, and for this I apologize to the reader.

1

You Are Infinitely More Than You Think

My one regret in life is that I am not someone else.
—WOODY ALLEN

WHEN I WAS A KID I was a real loser. At least, that is how I felt about myself. I was short and had curly red hair. Kids made fun of me and called me "carrot top." The only comeback I had was that the tops of carrots are green. I also had flat feet and had to wear corrective boots that looked really stupid. For kids, external things are very challenging, and I was the only one in my class with these stupid-looking boots. To make it worse, boys are expected to be real sportsmen, and sports were definitely not my thing. When the class was picking soccer teams, I'd hear them argue, "You take him . . . No, you take him." They used to call me crazy legs because when I played, I would sometimes miss the ball and kick the nearest guy in the ankle.

Although I felt like such a loser, deep inside I knew that I was not. I recall seeing the movie *Funny Girl,* starring Barbara Streisand. It was about a young woman struggling to become a star, but she came across like a real loser and a klutz. She sang a song that struck a deep chord within me about how she knew inside that she was a great star. I felt that was true for me too and today I know that it is true for everyone because we are all souls and there is no such thing as a loser soul. Why not? Because the soul that is the real you—your true self—is none other than an individualized expression of God—the Soul of souls, the Great Self.

Most people think that God is some super being floating in another realm called heaven, watching us from above. When the first Russian cosmonaut Yuri Gagarin went into space, ground control asked him, "What do you see?" He answered, "I don't see God."

What did he think he would see? Did he think that somewhere along his journey he would get to the edge of space and there would be two huge eyes peering at him? "Hi, I'm God. What took you so long?"

A lot of people think this way, but this is not what the Torah and Kabbalah teach. God does not exist in heaven while we exist on Earth—separate and far apart from him. God is not a "someone over there." Rather God is the One—the Only One, and each and every one of us is a "someone"—some of that One. We are each an aspect of God—a unique expression of the Great Self. If we were to compare God to the sun, each of us would be a ray of his light. Every single one of us yearns to feel like a rare, precious, and cherished masterpiece because in truth each and every one of us is indeed a piece of the Master. And God loves each of us as he does his very self because we are a part of him. But why don't we feel that truth about ourselves? Why don't we treat ourselves and each other in ways that befit our divine greatness?

The Kabbalah teaches that when the soul comes into the world it forgets who it really is and who it's a part of. We then think, speak, and act in ways that do not suit our true selves as expressions of God. We adopt a persona that does not fit us. The Talmud teaches that we are so powerful that we, like God, could actually create worlds but our misdeeds stifle our potential.[1] This is the meaning of the prophetic message of, "But your wrongdoings have made a separation between you and your God."[2] In other words, if we were to live up to who we really are we would discover that we are fully tapped into divine wisdom, creativity, and power. In fact the Talmud records that one sage created a person but because this sage was not yet completely pure and true to his

Ultimate Self his creation was flawed and incapable of hearing and responding to others. However, there were two sages who every Friday afternoon created a calf for their Sabbath meals.

Our wisdom, creativity, and powers are all rooted in and drawn from God. However our ability to access these powers depends on how much our lifestyle and character expresses our innermost self. Character, which is like a garment to the soul, is woven out of our thought patterns, words, and deeds. Does our character suit the greatness of ourselves as expressions of God? Does it enable our true Self as a soul to shine with divine radiance?

The Me I Want to Be

At first glance this phrase seems ridiculous. Who is the Me I want to be? How could I not be me? And if I am not me, which seems kind of crazy, then why am I not me? Who is the Me that I am, and what is holding me back from being the Me that I want to be?

Only a human being struggles with a question like that. Animals for sure don't. Animals are just exactly who they are. They never regret who they are, and they have no aspirations to be other than who they already are. Have you ever seen a dog trying to be a cat? Or a cat looking at a dog with envy, because the dog can bark and he can't?

Unique to the human mind there exists a possible conflict between who I am and who I could be or should be. We sense a distinction between our self and our character. This duality can create tremendous stress and even much psychic pain in our lives. However, to overcome whatever is holding us back from becoming the me we want to be, we must clarify the difference between the Self and the Me.

Let's start with understanding the self. Did you ever play a kind of mind game as a child and ask yourself: "Who would I have been if my mother had married another man?" If you have asked yourself this question, it is because on some deep intuitive level you sensed you *could* have been somebody else. You sensed that your inner self would be the same you, but it would be playing a different character. You sensed that there is a Self that stands independent of a particular Me. You sensed that the Self is immutable, but the particular character, the Me, is not.

In a sweet little book called *Children's Letters to God*, I found a letter that was particularly humorous: "Dear God, if after death you send me back, please don't send me back as Jennifer Horton. Because I hate her guts."[3] Now how does a child intuit that she could come back and play another character?

In Kabbalah, there is much discussion about reincarnation and how we may return numerous times to this world playing a different character in each life. Each of us may have been on Earth in an earlier lifetime, playing a different Me—a different character. For instance, the Kabbalah teaches that the soul that played Abel, who was killed by his brother Cain, returned in a later life to play the character Noah, and then returned again to play Moses.

It works a bit like casting roles in a play. An actor, who has been scripted to play a death scene, gives himself over completely to the part and dies in the most convincing way on stage. But he gets up when the curtain closes and lives to embrace a new role in a new show. Shakespeare was not far off when he wrote: "All the world is a stage and all the men and women merely players."

You and I are like actors, and when we come into this world, we are given a part to play. But don't confuse the Self (the soul) with the Me (the character), the part you play.

I know that I am playing a role, a character who is a rabbi, who lives in Jerusalem, who is married, who has seven children and four grandchildren, and so forth. I know the Me who is this character. But there is an aspect of who I am—my Self—that transcends this character. When I describe Me, I am describing my persona, my character, but I am not describing my Self. I have a role to play, but I am not that role, I am not that character.

The legendary actor Kirk Douglas shared with me a story that clearly illustrates this kind of confusion. Kirk was known for playing the tough guy, the macho man, the cowboy, and so forth.

Looking for a challenge, he decided to play the struggling, sensitive artist Vincent Van Gogh in a movie called *Lust for Life*. This part was far out of character for Kirk at that time in his acting career. When the news broke, he immediately got a call from his old acting buddy John Wayne:

"Kirk, what's this I'm hearing about you? What's a cowboy like you doing with a sissy part like Van Gogh?"

Surprised by the comment, Kirk responded, "John, I've got news for you—we are not cowboys, we're actors."

When we remember that we, too, are like actors then each and every one of us has the power to be the Me we truly want to be.

To try to keep this straight, let's define our terms:

- There is the Me, which is ego consciousness. It is the character we play, and it includes our psychological clothing—such as our thoughts and feelings—and the physical sensations of our body. The fabric of our character is woven out of our thinking, speaking, and behavioral patterns.
- Then there is the Self, that is, the soul—a ray of God, so to speak. This is the conscious self, the knower, the actor who plays the character. We will discuss later how, in fact, this self has two competing aspects that long to be integrated. One aspect—we'll call it the creative self—works through the character, utilizing its strengths and weaknesses, and seeks to advance forward to fulfill its creative mission on Earth. The second aspect—we'll call it the sacred self—yearns to retreat inward to experience its eternal connection to its divine source.
- And then there is the "I," who is the Great I, the Ultimate Self, the Soul of souls—God. Of course, when we say, "I am," it is not God, the Great I, speaking. It might be the Self, or the soul (a ray of the Great I) speaking, but most often it is just Me, the ego.

The question is what type of Me is worth wanting to be. The Me we want to be is a Me that enables our Self to shine out as an expression of the Great I.

The Me I Don't Want to Be

I was on a plane a couple of months ago, flipping through a magazine, when I saw an ad for plastic surgery. This particular ad had a list of every available procedure and how much it would cost, complete with an easy credit payment. I took out my calculator and figured out what it would cost to get a whole new me. I could move my eyebrows and ears higher or lower and move my cheeks and chin backward or forward. There were procedures that I could not imagine people wanting to get, like a bigger bottom. Why would anyone want a bigger rear end? What's wrong with the one I already have? You could also get fatter lips. As a kid I used to buy plastic lips as a joke, and they were certainly much cheaper than getting surgery. I was shocked to discover that in order to get fatter lips, the surgeon injects into your lips cells scraped from cadavers, dead bodies. Why would anyone want to kiss such a person? It's the kiss of death.

To become the Me I want to be I need to first determine what is wrong with the Me I already am. I then need to decide what kind of Me is worth wanting to be.

Sometimes we feel that the way we are coming across does not "fit"—our behavior and our mannerisms do not reveal our true godly self. Since the Self is the soul and the Me is the character we play or the psychological clothing we wear, the Me we want to be should be a character that enables the true inner beauty of the soul to really shine as an expression of our Ultimate Self—God.

Sometimes the Me we are playing simply doesn't feel right. We feel like an actor who is uncomfortable with a particular role he has been scripted to play. Or we feel like we are wearing clothing that doesn't fit right. It might be the right size, but it feels uncomfortable because it does not enable our real Self—our unique, brilliant, resilient, warm, awesome, miraculous Self—to shine. And sometimes we sew together psychological clothing cut from patterns of thinking, speaking, and acting that just don't fit us and reveal us. Each of us cannot feel happy with our Me when it's just a cover up and does not reveal the greatness of our true godly self.

I once saw a humorous comic strip called *Fifth St.* that featured an unhappy fellow going out on a date. He was pictured looking in the mirror, while his mother commented: "What's wrong? You have on a Tommy Hilfiger shirt, Calvin Klein pants, and Michael Jordan shoes. Now go out there and be yourself!"

Your garment is never your essence; the clothes you wear are not you, they are *on* you. Similarly, your character, behavioral patterns, and mannerisms are not you. You can never change yourself; you do not need to and you shouldn't want to because there is nothing wrong with the essential you. You are a soul. And as a soul you are nothing less than a unique expression of God. But it may be that your psychological clothing is not your size. It doesn't fit you because you are a soul and souls are always extra large. Small, petty, negative thoughts, talk, and deeds don't fit your greatness. And those you can change—you must change—if you want the real you to shine out.

Dying to Change

In a very powerful teaching, the Talmud tells us that we will not succeed in tapping the wisdom of God until we kill ourselves for it.[4] Since the Talmud also forbids suicide, this might seem like a crazy statement at first glance until we consider its real meaning in terms of personal transformation—the dynamics of empowerment, growth, and change.

Think of it this way: If you were a seed and you wanted to grow, you would have to be willing to die as a seed to become a tree. If you refuse to let go of your identity as a seed, then your growth—your life—is over. If you were a caterpillar and you wanted to become a butterfly, you would have to let yourself as a caterpillar die so that you could emerge from your cocoon, fly, and be a butterfly.

In other words, when you are ready to play a bigger part, take on a greater role, and live a life of dynamic growth guided by the wisdom of God, you must be willing to die and be born anew in each moment. When you think about it, you will realize that you have already died a number of times in this life. I am certain that you and every person alive could come up with a list of characters that we have already played in this lifetime but that are no longer alive.

But so many of us are stuck in the past, playing characters that we need to let die, so that we can get on with life and let our souls shine with the divine radiance of the Great I. Too many of us are living self-fulfilled prophecies about ourselves. We think we are victims. We think we are losers. We are like a broken record constantly repeating to ourselves in our heads and even sometimes out loud to others, "I'm lazy," "I'm stupid," "I'm ugly." But it's impossible to be a lazy, stupid, or ugly soul. Souls are always and only energetic, brilliant, and beautiful. It's just that we are not acting out who we really are inside.

One day as I was strolling in a park I heard a mother yelling at her son calling him "a stupid piece of monkey." Poor fellow, he did not even merit to be a whole monkey, just a stupid piece of monkey. I saw the shame on the child's face. How cruel. This woman needed to understand that if her son starts swinging from trees and eating bananas, she did it. She did it because she convinced her child that he is a stupid piece of monkey. Hopefully, this boy will grow to know that he is a masterpiece, so to speak, a piece of God, and that it was only his mother that drove him ape. Hopefully, he will have the courage to let go of the monkey business of low self-esteem and reveal the godly brilliance of his soul.

It's been said that you have to be willing to sacrifice who you are in this moment to become who you can be in the future. Therefore, the only thing holding you back from being the Me that you can be—the Me that enables your godly self to shine—is you. Nobody else.

The soul, the real you, is brilliant, powerful, miraculous. You are no less than an individualized expression of God, a manifestation of God. The time has come to courageously kill the petty character that is burying your incredible light.

The Talmud also teaches that if an assassin is after you to kill you, you should kill him first.[5] Sometimes your character is so narrow and small minded that it is choking your soul to death—your character is killing you. In that case, not only are you allowed to kill your character, you *must* kill it so that your true self can live.

Decide who is the Me that you want to be and get rid of the Me or the aspect of your Me that is murdering your soul, disconnecting you from the Great I. The only real things holding you back from happiness, growth, and lasting change are your beliefs. What you believe about yourself determines how you act and feel around others.

Don't underestimate the power of your beliefs. It can even affect the way you look. For instance, until I was twenty-six years old, I had a little space between my two front teeth. And as we all know, in the world of perfect dentistry, this is unacceptable. So I felt self-conscious about it. One day I mentioned this to my wife. She told me that in Tunis, which is where she grew up, a space between your two front teeth is a sign of great luck. It was one of the first things she noticed about me when we were dating, and she found it attractive. A couple of months after this revealing discussion with my wife, I noticed that the space actually disappeared. To me that was God's way of telling me that all I needed to do is to change my beliefs. And, indeed, I now realize that the space between my teeth was a sign of luck—I consider myself lucky to have learned about the power of my beliefs.

Believe that you can change. Believe in your godly greatness. Believe that the Me you don't want to be can die, and a new Me can be born that lets your soul come alive as an expression of the Great I.

Summary

You are infinitely more than you think because you are none other than an individualized expression of God—the Great I, the

Ultimate Self. God is not a super being floating in another realm called heaven. He is not someone over there whom we exist apart from. Each of us is a part of God—a unique expression of God. If we were to compare God to the sun, each of us would be a ray of his light. When the soul comes into the world it forgets who it really is and who it is really a part of. We might then think, speak, and act in ways that do not suit our true selves as expressions of God—ways that numb our ability to feel our divine greatness. It is only our flawed lifestyle that separates us from God and stifles our godly potential. However, the more we live up to who we really are, the more we tap into God's wisdom, creativity, love, power, and goodness.

Each of us is like an actor playing a role. Our goal is to play a character (Me) that enables our true self to shine out as an expression of the Great I, the Ultimate Self. Small, petty, negative thoughts, talk, and deeds don't fit us. But all that we can change. We must change if we want to experience and celebrate the greatness of our true self. When we are ready to play a bigger part, take on a greater godly role, we must be free to transcend our persona and let the character we don't want to play anymore die. To take on a new part we have to learn to let go of ego and set our soul free to come alive as an expression of the Ultimate I.

2

The Journey from Ego to Soul

I ONCE WENT TO A GYM to improve my respiratory health. I wanted to exercise, and I figured it was best to put myself in a supportive environment. I didn't know that the gym I chose specialized in body building. When I walked in, I saw a bunch of guys pumping iron. The entire place was wall-to-wall mirrors so that the bodybuilders could constantly look at themselves. I never saw such huge muscles in my life. They could even flex their earlobes!

After taking in the scene, I said to the owner (a muscle-bound fellow himself), "Why would I want to spend my time doing this? What would I get out of it?"

He said to me, "Listen, when I was a teenager, I was a scrawny little runt with no confidence. Then I went into bodybuilding, and I got confidence. When you walk out of here after you've worked out, and you're all puffed up, the ladies are gonna look at you, man. And you're gonna feel real good."

I just looked at him and said, "I'm a rabbi. Being puffed up is not what I'm looking for." I found it very interesting that this man's physique was the source of his self. He once had a weak sense of self, and his solution was to build his body. But I really don't believe that he now has a strong sense of self. I'm sure he *feels* a strong sense of self, but as he watches his body begin to deteriorate with time, and as he faces death in whatever way he will face it, he is going to question his true identity and self-worth.

Suspended between the Me and the "Great I," we are in a quandary and we must make a choice. Our dilemma is to either seek personal value through our ego or through identifying with God. Will we choose to seek our self-worth through identifying with our character—our opinions, emotions, actions, accomplishments, talents, profession, social status, fame, money, property, physique? Or will we seek to identify with God—experience ourselves rooted in the Great I and serve to channel into the world God's wisdom, creativity, love, and goodness?

Identity is acquired through a process of identification. If a person identifies with his money, and money has value to him, then he feels he has value. As we know, society places an extremely high value on money. That's why people struggle to accumulate money and those who succeed delude themselves into thinking that they are now very valuable. And all that is fine as long as they are wealthy. But when they lose their wealth, and we all eventually do because you can't take it with you, then they will feel as if they have lost their self.

There is a story about a man who so totally identified with his wealth that, in preparing for his eventual death, he arranged for his brother to bury him with all his money. His brother promised to carry out the man's wishes.

Overhearing the exchange, a friend said to the brother, "You must be crazy! Are you really going to bury him with all his money?"

"I certainly will," the brother said. "I made a commitment."

When the man died, it came time for the brother to fill the coffin with all the deceased's money. Yet at the funeral, the friend noticed that there were no bills surrounding the body. Inside lay only one little note.

"Where is all the cash?" the friend asked the brother, reminding him that he had promised to fulfill the dead man's wishes. "I expected to see wheelbarrows full of dollars in this coffin."

"No, no," the brother said. "I have it all worked out. I wrote him a check for $3 million, put it in his coffin, and took all the money. I'm good for it."

I am not saying that there is anything about our persona that is innately bad. The Torah instructs us to respect our persona, develop our thoughts, nurture our talents, take care of our bodies, and enjoy our material wealth. In fact the Torah teaches that among the various prerequisites to attain prophecy the prophet must be wise, strong, and wealthy. Our persona expresses our soul and is like a garment. We must simply be careful never to think that our persona is the *source* of our true inner self-worth.

Abraham used his money to do acts of kindness and give charity, helping people see that they, too, could serve God with their money. But money was never the source of his self-worth or his identity. Throughout his life, serving God's purpose was the source of Abraham's identity.

If we identify too closely with the character we play, if we are always seeking to derive our sense of self from our persona, then we are investing in something very transient. The character you play is temporary—here today, gone tomorrow.

This is why death is shocking to most people. It's unfathomable to many how someone who, just yesterday, was the head of the government, influencing international events, and the next day could be gunned down and killed by a rebellious teenager. Death shocks us into facing how easily our persona can be obliterated.

King Solomon imparted this exact lesson when he declared, "I praise the living dog over the dead king."[1] Though we may appear majestic amid all our outer trappings, our glory means nothing if we are not alive to put them to good use.

If we choose to make our persona the source of our identity and self-worth, then certainly we are right to fear that we will die, since all this will certainly pass away. But we need not be afraid at all. If we identify with God, and affirm that only God is the source of our self-worth, we will experience the immortality of our soul. And we understand that our persona is meant to be an expression or garment of the soul but not its source of worth.

Eternally You

Rooted in God the soul remains forever stable. It is the axis upon which the persona revolves. Get a picture of yourself when you were five years old, with ice cream drooling down your chin and chocolate all over your face, and ask yourself, "Is that me?" You may change day by day, yet there remains that core you, the never-changing self who animates the ever-changing persona. You, as a soul, remain the same in good times and bad times, in times of joy and sadness, pain and pleasure, celebration and mourning.

King Solomon wore a ring engraved with the dictum, "This too shall pass." It reminded him that both times of trouble and times of happiness would not last forever. Amid the ever-changing times and the conflicting moods of the people, King Solomon acknowledged that his soul is permanently anchored in God.

If your soul is not anchored in God then you will be caught in the current of your persona and mistakenly think that you will always feel the way you are currently feeling. In other words, when you are feeling good, you will think that you had always felt good and will always feel good. Then, when bad times come knocking on your door, you are devastated and have great difficulty bouncing back. Likewise, when you are feeling down, you will feel that you have always been down and will stay that way forever. When a new opportunity for joy appears, you will have to grope and grapple to embrace it.

I often see this problem with people who attend my seminars. Suddenly, they feel empowered and elated, certain that they can take on the world. They identify with their present mood and mistakenly think they are this mood. It's a common problem. We all think, "I am happy," rather than, "I am feeling happy right now, but I have felt sad at other times and I know that I will probably feel sad in the future. I am feeling sad right now, but there have been many times when I was feeling happy, and there will be future times when I will feel happy again."

But King Solomon knew the secret. He understood that while

these thoughts and feelings will pass, the soul and its connection to God will never pass. After all, we exist only because God exists. When Moses asked God his name, God answered *Ahiyeh Asher Ahiyeh*—"I am because I am." Only God can say that. Only God is a self-sustaining Self. We cannot say, "I am because I am." We must acknowledge the truth that, "I am because God is." If there was no eternal "I am" who created us and sustains us as an expression of himself, then we would not exist.

Descartes said, "I think, therefore I am." The Torah teaches, "God is, therefore I am." We desire immortality because we are immortal souls—expressions of the Immortal One. This explains why we intuit an incredible sense of connection to a greater whole because in our essence we are a part of that greater whole. But if we don't acknowledge that truth and think, speak, and act in ways that deny it then we become estranged to ourselves and create our own spiritual exile.

Set Your Soul Free

At the beginning of the Book of Ezekiel, the prophet declares, "I was among the exiled."[2] The *Zohar* explains that Ezekiel's words had a double meaning. He was referring not only to his individual self but also to the "Great I." In other words, when Ezekiel was exiled—when his personal "I" was in exile—he knew that an aspect of God was also in exile, because he knew that his true self was rooted in God and that he was actually a unique individualized expression of God.

The twentieth-century Kabbalist rabbi Aryeh Kaplan explains in his book *Inner Space* that in order to feel this powerful truth, we must be free to disengage our Self from its outer trappings. In other words, we must get in touch with our soul as distinct from our Me—our persona, thoughts, feelings, and mannerisms—and be free to act out of character if need be.

We often become what we think, feel, and do. When this happens, it is difficult for us to distinguish the thought from the thinker, the feeling from the feeler, and the deed from the doer. We are then a prisoner and slave to our persona rather than a free soul and a master. A person who becomes so angry that he loses control becomes one with his anger. But, in truth, he is not his anger—he is just *feeling* anger so intensely that the borders of what he feels and who he is are blurred. He then becomes a slave to his anger and uncontrollably acts it out.

Have you ever gone into a furious rage and yet experienced yourself above the anger, as if simultaneously watching yourself yelling or breaking something and wondering why you're doing it? Have you ever broken down in tears, yet somehow also felt yourself outside the storm of emotions knowing that you were going to come out of this pain, going to get through it?

These paradoxical moments—when you are in the midst of your emotions and actions yet outside of them—are times when you realize that thinking, feeling, and doing are distinct from your inner self. There is a distinction between you as the knower and actor and your knowledge and actions, between you as the one who experiences and the experience itself. But because the knowing and acting subject and the knowledge and action are closely connected, we often forget about, and lose touch with, the difference between them.

During Isralight Shabbat dinners, I encourage people to close their eyes and sing with me the special melodies of Shabbat. To help them relax, I intentionally have the lights dimmed. I find that when the lights are bright, the participants feel that others are looking at them and are then less prone to let go and experience the soulful Shabbat spirit. But, even with the mood lighting and encouragement, there are still some people who are afraid to close their eyes.

One Shabbat participant said that he did not see the point of closing his eyes because when he did, all he saw was "nothing." I told him that seeing "nothing" was precisely what I wanted him to achieve. We are so involved with what we see that we lose touch with ourselves as the "seer." By closing our eyes and letting go, we can distinguish the seer from the seen. But for some people, seeing nothing means they will be left with nothing.

The goal of freeing yourself from the outer trappings is to realize that your thoughts, your emotions, your actions, your looks, your money, your career, your property, and so on are not you. They may accurately express you, or they may not. They are part of your outer trappings. They make up the fabric of your psychological clothing, and they may fit you well, enabling the greatness of your godliness to shine out. Or they may not fit. And even if they do fit you well they may not fit you well on all occasions.

Many people fear, however, that if they were to strip themselves of these externals, make changes, and try on something new they would end up feeling like they had lost themselves. If that is their attitude then indeed they have already lost themselves in their persona. They are in spiritual exile. To prevent your persona from becoming a prison you must experience your inner self stripped of its outer trappings.

Viktor Frankl, the famed originator of logotherapy, gets this point across very dramatically in his book *Man's Search for Meaning*. He describes the selection process in a Nazi concentration camp—a Nazi commander standing at the front of the line of Jewish prisoners, holding up his hand and with one finger, simply pointing left, right, left, right. One man's finger determined whether a person would live or die.

Spared death, Frankl and others were sent into a room where they were ordered to strip naked and pile their clothes into the center of the room. The Jewish prisoners frantically undressed and threw their clothes and possessions in the central pile, fearful of running out of time and being killed. At the end, all they were left with was their naked existence.

Frankl, however, stood still holding his manuscripts, which contained a lifetime of research. That little bundle held everything that he had accomplished. Gripping his life's work, he approached the German officer and tried to explain that this was worth nothing to the Nazis. At first, the officer seemed to listen compassionately, but then yelled, "Throw it into the pile!" Frankl frantically persisted, "You don't understand. This is my life's work! It's just meaningless and worthless paper to you." But the Nazi repeated, "Throw it into the pile!" Frankl obeyed the order. He, too, was left with only his naked existence.

Imagine the tragedy of his loss. But also imagine the freedom and spiritual power that was suddenly made available to him. Sometimes, very painful experiences offer us quantum spiritual leaps. Frankl addresses this concept in his writings, relating how many people in the concentration camps became remarkably soulful. Those who were more religious and spiritually oriented, Frankl explains, lasted longer than those who were athletic, strong, and robust but lacked the inner strength of soul.

Frankl writes that after everyone had stripped, the Nazis gave out concentration camp uniforms, which were previously worn by someone who had just died in a gas chamber. As Frankl put on the torn, dirty prison uniform, he reached into the pocket and found a tiny piece of paper. He took it out and saw that it was the text of the *Shema,* the Jews' daily declaration that God is absolutely the One and Only. This little piece of a prayer book that another Jew had managed to keep was Frankl's exchange for his collection of manuscripts. Frankl realized that when he gave up his life's work, he got the *Shema.*

To me this means that when Frankl was stripped of his persona and left to confront his naked soul he was empowered to discover his true identity—to identify with the source of all self-worth, the one and only God, the Great I.

The Journey of the Soul

This is what Abraham accomplished when he responded to the call of God asking him, "Go forth from your country, from your birthplace, and from your father's house, to a land that I will show you. I will make you into a great nation, I will bless you and make you great."[3]

The Hebrew phrase *lech lecha,* which is generally translated as "go forth," literally means "go to yourself." But how was Abraham to accomplish this when he was simultaneously being told to abandon the basic elements of his identity—his country, birthplace, and parents' home? God was asking Abraham to free himself from his limiting identity so that he could take a spiritual journey toward a *new* identity, which would reveal his true self rooted in God.

This is clear from the peculiar order of the instructions. To start out on a ordinary physical journey, Abraham would chronologically first leave his father's house, then the city of his birth, and finally the border of his country, but here the order is inverted: "Go forth from your country, your birthplace, and your father's house . . ." Obviously, this was no mere relocation. This was a journey toward a new identity, and therefore, the sequence of departure was given in the progressive order of psychological difficulty of severing attachments.

Unlike most people, whose identity is rooted in their nationality, land, and family, Abraham was asked to go beyond his persona, transcend his Me. He had to let go of all that was familiar and embrace a new sense of self that was rooted in the Great Self. When God told him, "I will make you into a great nation, I will bless you and make you great," the message was clear: "I, God, will be the source of your power and light."

Mark Twain, who was not Jewish, once wrote: "All things are mortal, but the Jew; all other forces pass, but he remains. What is the secret of his immortality?"[4] The answer to Mark Twain's question lies in God's instruction to Abraham, which is the secret of how the Jews would survive two thousand years of exile from their land. Because their identity never depended on the country they lived in, they survived as a nation even though they were scattered over the face of the Earth. Because their identity was not confined to simple nationalism, they survived thousand of years of exile from their homeland. And finally, because their identity even transcended familial attachments they survived the

Holocaust when whole families were decimated leaving solitary survivors. Jewish identity, as defined by the patriarch Abraham, is founded upon identification with the immortal—the Eternal I, God.

Lech lecha—the process of going to yourself—was only the first step of Abraham's transformational journey. Each event in his life was a new challenge to go beyond his persona, transcend his character, and affirm his connection to God. The Kabbalah teaches that Abraham was the epitome of kindness. Yet when we review the story of his life, we find that this gentle, caring, loving man was repeatedly challenged to act out of character and behave in a manner that can only be described as harsh and unkind.

First, he had to leave his aging father. Then, he had to instruct his nephew Lot to go away from him and set up house elsewhere for the sake of peace. Next, he had to go to war to save Lot, who was in danger. Then, at age ninety, God requested that he circumcise himself. Then, God commanded him to cut ties with a part of his family—his son Ishmael and Ishmael's mother Hagar—because they were undermining his divine mission on Earth. And to top it off, God asked him to sacrifice his son Isaac. All these acts require character traits contrary to loving-kindness. And indeed that is exactly the point. Abraham was able to transcend his character— to act out of character—and freely affirm his innermost self and reveal his profound identification with God—the Great Self.

Exercising Freedom

Who are we, after all? Are we a character or are we a soul, an individualized expression of God? If we can't let go of our persona, then we are its prisoner and slave. If the source of our identity is our opinions, actions, looks, career, money, property, social status and what others think of us, then we are not our selves. We are souls in exile, estranged from inner selves. The soul is not at home when it is disconnected from the Great I—its true source, ground, context, and essence.

To keep our souls in shape and stay spiritually fit we need to exercise our freedom daily. We need to reclaim our inner self and redirect it to God. The great Hassidic master Rabbi Kalonymous Kalman Shapira, who was the rabbi of the Warsaw Ghetto during the Holocaust, taught a powerful and special meditation he called Inner Silence.

You start off by simply observing your thoughts. You're not supposed to think of anything specific, you just let your mind go free and watch the thoughts that appear across the screen of your mind. Suddenly, you'll discover how bombarded your mind is with thoughts. As Rabbi Shapira explained, the only difference between you and a madman is that a madman actually goes along with all his random thoughts. A sane person, however, can just watch the stream of thoughts go by and not get caught up in them. When you do this silent watching, you begin to sense the distinction between yourself as the knowing subject, and the knowledge—the distinction between you and your ideas.

Once you reach this stage of awareness—when you have distinguished yourself from your knowledge and experienced yourself as a soul distinct from your persona—choose a verse from the Torah and repeat it in your mind. According to Jewish tradition Moses the prophet was completely tuned in to the Great I and therefore the words of the Torah are the words and thoughts of God. By meditating on a verse from the Torah you can become conscious of your connection to God who is the supreme knowing subject—the Soul of Souls.

This exercise empowers you to get a handle on your life. When you take a step back, look at your ego from outside yourself, and experience yourself plugged into God, you can then begin to take control of your life.

When the Jewish people encountered God at Mt. Sinai and received the commandments, they consciously plugged into the Great I. In so doing, they experienced the difference between freedom *from* oppression and freedom *to* expression. After they were freed *from* Egyptian slavery, they were freed at Mt. Sinai *to* be themselves and actualize themselves to serve as channels for the presence of God on Earth—to manifest divine wisdom, creativity, love, and goodness.

We, too, can be freed from being victimized by whatever enslaves us in life—be it our personal addictions, obsessions, bad habits, or attachments. But that alone does not guarantee us the freedom to be ourselves. This would be analogous to the Jewish people escaping Egypt but never receiving the commandments at Mt. Sinai and getting to the Promised Land. In other words, they would be left to wander in the desert, free from the oppression of Egypt, but they would have never achieved the freedom to be who they were meant to be.

To enjoy complete freedom, not just freedom *from* but also freedom *to,* we have to know who in essence we really are—who our eternal root is and what purpose we serve on Earth. An essential ingredient in the recipe for self-actualization is the ability to let go of ego and, when required, the freedom to act out of character. However, letting go of ego is not enough to empower us to fully anchor our souls in God and serve to make manifest God's presence on Earth. We must also learn to courageously confront our existential loneliness.

Summary

Our true strength and ultimate self-worth lies in knowing that each and every one of us is an individualized expression of God; a unique channel for his presence into this world. This is our ultimate purpose and joy. To live and feel this truth, however, we must be free to let go of ego and the outer trappings of our persona. Otherwise we are prisoners to our persona, disconnected and alienated from our inner self. Our soul suffers a self-imposed spiritual exile when we are trapped in our opinions, actions, career, body, money, property, social status, what others think of us, and everything else that makes up our character. Disengaging from our outer trappings, however, is not enough. This only accomplishes freedom *from* oppression. But to achieve freedom *to* expression we must identify with God—the Great Self—and serve as a channel for godly wisdom, creativity, love, power, and goodness. Until we reclaim our souls and connect to the divine source, ground, context, and essence of all, we are not at home. The prerequisite toward full self-actualization is the freedom to act out of character and anchor our souls in God, thinking, speaking, and acting in ways that serve to make manifest God's presence on Earth. But even this is only the first step. We must also learn to courageously face our existential loneliness.

3

From Alone to All One

WHETHER WE ARE single or married, have no friends, few friends, or many friends, we all still occasionally experience loneliness, even when we are surrounded by many people. In fact, we often experience some of our deepest feelings of loneliness at big social events.

Very often we are in denial about it because loneliness can be devastating. Yet strangely enough, it is precisely when we experience the depth of loneliness that we find God, we find each other, and we enjoy genuine companionship and profound love. As difficult as it may be to believe, loneliness plays a vital role in achieving full self-actualization. Paradoxically, embracing loneliness is the key to living a life of love, empowerment, fulfillment, and happiness anchored in the Great Self—God. Loneliness is actually a blessing. In fact the Torah records how Bilaam, one of the archenemies of the Jewish people, while intending to curse them ended up blessing them saying, "Verily, a people that will dwell alone."

Lonely Are the Free

The greatest spiritual leaders, whose stories are related in the Torah, were all lonely. Abraham was so alienated that people referred to him as the *Ivri,* meaning "the one from the other side."[1] He himself publicly affirmed, "I am a stranger and a sojourner among you."[2] Abraham's son Isaac was also an outsider. Although his father eventually became famous for his extraordinary religious ideas and generated a large following, Isaac nonetheless remained somewhat an unknown. He is described as the *Ish,* meaning "the person" or "the stranger."

Jacob, Isaac's son, was also lonely. After years of fleeing from his brother Esau, fearing that he would be killed by him, Jacob finally decided that he had to confront him. On his way to the confrontation, he turns back to the previous encampment to retrieve some pots that had been left behind. The verse then tells us, "And Jacob remained alone." The Midrash, the Oral tradition, associates this event with a verse in Deuteronomy that illuminates the deeper meaning behind Jacob's loneliness. The verse reads, "Who is like you God, (other than) Jeshurun?"[3] Jeshurun is another name for Jacob. The Midrash explains that just as it is written of God that "the Lord alone shall be exalted,"[4] so of Jacob it says: "And Jacob remained alone." In other words, Jacob and God are alike. They are alone. At that time, Jacob had a remarkable wrestling match with an angel who names Jacob "Israel," which means "he will rule as God." Interestingly, the *Zohar,* which explains the mystical meaning of the story, states: "The angel said to Jacob, 'We [the angels] now have to serve you, like we serve God.'"[5] In other words, when Jacob embraced and confronted his loneliness, he realized his incredible connection to and identification with God and became as godly as one could possibly be.

Abraham, Isaac, and Jacob were not the only lonely hearts in Torah history. Moses was certainly lonely, too. However, when we briefly take a look at his early life, we can easily see how rejection, alienation, and loneliness actually empowered him to master extraordinary prophetic powers and channel the very words of God.

Moses was born to an Israelite family while under the cruel oppression of the Egyptians. The pharaoh demanded that all newborn Israelite boys be killed. In desperation, Moses' mother put her baby in a basket and set it amongst the reeds along the banks of the Nile. The princess of Egypt, while bathing in the Nile, discovered the child, rescued him, and took him home to the palace. Ironically, she ends up unknowingly hiring Moses' mother to nurse this abandoned baby. Moses, therefore, received the royal upbringing of an Egyptian prince while always knowing that he was an Israelite. And indeed he was a restless soul. He yearned to share in the pain and sorrow of his brethren who were enslaved by the Egyptians. The first day he left the safe and luxurious confines of the palace, he encountered an Egyptian beating an Israelite. Without a moment of hesitation he killed the Egyptian. He quickly buried the body and returned to the palace. Even though Moses surely realized the grave implications of what he had done, the very next day Moses left the palace again. This time he saw an Israelite about to strike another Israelite.

Shocked and disturbed, he protested, "Why are you beating your brother?"

"Who appointed you as ruler and a judge over us?" the Israelite snapped with disdain. "Do you intend to murder me as you did the Egyptian?"[6]

Moses was devastated. Not only was he rejected by the people he selflessly helped, but his very own kin endangered his life by spreading the word about what he had done. The pharaoh immediately issued a death warrant and Moses had to flee from Egypt to the land of Midian. There he married a Midianite woman whose family, like himself, were outcasts, and he became a shepherd, caring for his father-in-law's flocks. And indeed, Moses named his first son Gershom (a combination of the Hebrew words "stranger" and "there") explaining, "I have been a stranger in a strange land."[7]

It was no coincidence that just after Moses spoke these heartbreaking words the Torah reports his initial encounter with God—the vision of the burning bush. Imagine his overwhelming loneliness. He was an Israelite rejected by his people and a prince of Egypt who was now a fugitive. Forced to abandon the luxuries of the royal palace, Moses becomes a simple shepherd.

Stripped of the trappings of ego and faced with the stark nakedness of his pure lonely self, Moses meets God. Identity crisis, abandonment, loneliness, and alienation all freed Moses and empowered him to discover his connection to the Great I—God.

Loneliness is a gift. Ironically, it is the very gateway to extraordinary companionship. All of us feel lonely at times. We can deny it or pretend that we are not feeling it, or we can embrace it and let the loneliness lead us to an intensely deep realization of our intimate connection and fellowship with God.

Never Alone

We have an incredible craving for uniqueness; a relentless drive to express our one and only irreplaceable self. But as soon as we achieve our greatest dream of uniqueness we feel defeated because we then have nothing in common with others. Now that we have asserted our uniqueness, we have no one to speak to.

If each of us is totally and completely unique, how can any of us understand the other? We each have our own language, our own experience, our own way. If people can understand us, then we are like them and therefore not 100 percent unique. And no matter what we share with others, if what we say comes from the deepest place of our uniqueness, then it comes from the deepest place of our loneliness. And with time that loneliness only becomes amplified and intensified. Because the older and more unique we get, the more we feel that nobody understands us. Yet we do this to ourselves. We work hard to become unique, creative, special, novel, and original only to discover, strangely enough, that our very accomplishment creates another problem for us.

This problem often starts with our parents as we are growing up. Initially as children we feel one with our parents. Because we do not understand the boundaries of selfhood, we are certain that our mother and father feel our pain. Our boo-boo is their boo-boo. But as we grow more mature and become more Self-conscious and aware of our uniqueness we start to feel abandoned by our parents. Suddenly it hits us that they do not understand us. They do not really know what we are feeling. They do not feel what we are feeling. They do not see things quite how we see them.

Once we feel this loneliness, we begin to realize that our pain is different from other people's pain. And even though people often say, "I know how you feel," they really do not know how we feel. They think they know how we feel, because they may have had *similar* experiences, but they could not have gone through our exact personal experience. Conversely, we cannot know how they feel. And no matter how very similar our experiences may be we are still not the one going through the other's present pain.

When I share my pain with you I cannot expect you to *feel* my pain. Because you are not me. Yet you do feel something. With your memory you are accessing your own pain, which you hope approximates my pain, but it is still not my pain. In so much that it is my pain, I am totally alone. In so much that it is my joy, I am totally alone. And no matter what you say to me, it is still my pain and not yours.

This applies to all of us. Simply because we are unique, we are totally alone—unless something miraculous happens, and we have the guts to completely face and embrace our loneliness. Then, paradoxically, we experience the most profound sense of loving fellowship and compassionate companionship. Because in the depths of our loneliness, in the depths of our uniqueness, we meet God. From within the intensity of loneliness we can experience the eternal connection and intimate identification of our individual I with the Ultimate I—God.

This is the deeper meaning behind the touching words of the psalmist: "A Song of the Ascents. From out of the depths I called You, God."[8] In other words, from the depths of our innermost unique self we call to God. And we know that he compassionately hears our call because there is no infinite gap that separates us. He is not in some far-off celestial realm. Rather he is the Soul of our soul; our root, ground, essence, and context. He is the Self of all selves, our Supreme Self. And therefore the Torah teaches that God feels our pain. Isaiah the prophet asserted: "In all their afflictions He was afflicted."[9] The Book of Psalms states: ". . . I am with him in his pain."[10] There we also read, "Even if I walk in the valley of death I will not fear evil because You are with me."[11] The *Zohar,* the chief work of the Kabbalah, interprets this psalm literally. God is completely with us in the valley of death. The Talmud makes a similar claim, stating that when we are hurting, the Divine Presence is at our side[12]—God actually feels our pain.

Even the people closest to us in our life cannot feel our pain, so we feel lonely. But if we embrace that pain something amazing happens—we hit the bedrock of loneliness, and mysteriously, we get a deep and thrilling clarity that we are never alone. And we too realize what the psalmist expressed so well: "Though my mother and my father have abandoned me, God will take me in."[13] God is involved with us constantly, feeling our feelings, sharing our pain, and sharing our joys. Oddly enough within the very depth of loneliness we discover that we are in truth never alone.

Ecstasy in a Heartbeat

It is one thing to intellectually understand that we are never alone, that God is with us even in our most painful moments. But how can we know and feel this truth experientially?

Let me share with you how this truth hit me like a ton of bricks when I was a teenager. It happened while I was having a tense and upsetting discussion with my father. He expressed his strong disapproval of my very free and haphazard adolescent lifestyle and told me that it was about time I took responsibility and made some serious changes. His challenging and persistent rap became more and more annoying until my ego couldn't take it any longer and I angrily shouted, "This is my life and I can do with it as I please!" I stomped out of the room, slammed the door, and threw myself on my bed. As I lay there I became very aware of my throbbing heart, beating intensely from the outburst of my emotions. I wondered, "What makes me so sure this is my life? Is this me beating my heart? If I'm beating my heart then I should be able to turn it off and on at will." I then began to wonder about my ability to breathe, digest, think, feel, move, etc. I wondered, "Are these powers all mine? In fact, are any of the powers within me, from me?"

Think about it. Even if we tried, we could not force ourselves to stop thinking. It's impossible. But, if we cannot stop thinking, is it really us who is doing the thinking? If it were, we should be free to take a break and stop our minds. Who then is thinking our thoughts? Of course what we think is our choice, but the fact that we think at all is not our choice.

Similarly, we can't stop feeling. We can choose what to feel but we cannot choose whether or not *to* feel. If we cannot stop feeling or start feeling at will, then we are not really the masters of our feelings. Who, then, is the master?

Although we have a body, and we have some control over it— we can tell it to sit still, go to sleep, run a marathon—but there is a great deal about the body that we do not control. We can't tell it to digest or secrete sweat. There are seventeen facial muscles that must work in perfect coordination for every syllable to come out of our mouths. Do *we* do that? Did we invent this marvelous co-ordination? Are we the source and master of this power? What we say is our choice. But does the power of speech belong to us?

This is also true for our will in general. We can choose what we want, but we cannot choose whether or not *to* want. Choice is not a choice. Ironically free choice is forced upon us. *What* we choose is our choice, but *that* we choose is not our choice.

So who is telling our emotions to feel? And who is fueling our minds to think? Who is infusing us with willpower? And who is beating our hearts? I suggest we stay in good contact with who-ever that is.

Kabbalah teaches that this great "whoever" is who we are refer-ring to when we say God. Most people think we can't see God be-cause he is so far away in some other realm. But the real reason we can't see God is because he is too close; closer than our very own eyeballs. God is the Master Self. He is the Soul of our soul, and we are one with him—although not the same as him. There is a distinction between God and us, just as there is a distinction between the sun and its rays, but there is no separation. And therefore, God is involved with us constantly, feeling our feelings, thinking our thoughts, and living our lives.

Partners Forever

With a little contemplation it becomes self-evident that the raw materials of our lives—will, thought, feelings, mobility, and vitality—are not ours. All the essential powers of life that we think we own are really on loan. We didn't invent them or create them. They do not start with us nor end with us. The powers within us are not from us but we *do* give them their form. We choose to make our will into good will or bad will. We decide whether we think up loving thoughts or ones that are hateful. It is up to us to speak healing words or hurtful words. We determine whether our actions build or destroy. Our ability to think, feel, and do is God's choice but *what* we think, feel, and do is our choice. Life is a partnership between us and God. God provides the raw materials, or the basic substance, and we decide what form they will take in this world.

A friend of mine who is a very successful artist once asked me to take one of his paintings to the United States. I said to him, "When I get to the border, I'll have to declare its value."

"It's worth about $50," he told me.

"What are you talking about? Your paintings go for about $5,000 to $10,000!"

"No," he said, "they're really only worth $50 in materials. The form that I give to them cannot be valued."

Now that was really interesting. A person can take inexpensive canvas and paints, give them new form, and all of a sudden you have an original art piece worth thousands of dollars.

We, too, give life its form and determine its value for us. God creates and provides us with the raw powers of life but as his partners we determine their form. Daily living is a human/divine enterprise of shared thinking, feeling, and doing. And when we realize that and live up to that truth we reclaim our godly worth and experience heaven on Earth.

King David writes in the Book of Psalms: "If I would ascend to heaven, You are there; if I would make my bed in hell, You are there as well."[14]

This is a strange verse. After all, what is God doing in hell? King David is telling us metaphorically that God is with us wherever we go. There is no separation between God and us even if we are in hell. God provides the substance of life, and we provide its form. And together we enjoy a loving partnership. The human/divine covenant is a relationship of unconditional love. It is a bond that can never be broken but it can be forgotten. When we forget our eternal connection to God life feels like hell. But when we live and celebrate our oneness with God that experience itself is heaven.

Our intimate connection with God is a constant but we must acknowledge and live it to feel it. However, to experience this truth in its fullest sense we must embrace the depths of absolute aloneness. And when we courageously do that, we mysteriously meet our Ultimate Life Partner. We then discover, paradoxically, that we are not alone at all. Precisely when we face our inner incommunicable uniqueness and embrace our existential loneliness, we encounter a profound communion and companionship with God. We feel connected to the Great Other who is not us and yet completely one with us. The painful feeling of being alone is miraculously transformed into a loving feeling of being all one with God and the rest of the world.

True Love

In the depth of loneliness, we actually meet each other and find true love. Although we are unique and different in form we are one in substance. Even though our bodies separate us we are one with each other because we are all connected to God—the Soul of souls. In God we discover our one shared Universal Self.

The Talmud teaches that a man and a woman who do not have God in their marriage will not have a lasting relationship. We can see this concept in the Hebrew words for "man" and "woman." *Ish,* man, and *isha,* woman, are nearly identical words; however, one has the letter *yud* and the other the letter *hei.* Joined together, these letters spell one of the names of God. However, if you take these letters away, what is left spells *eish* meaning fire. Therefore, Torah teaches, if you take God out of marriage all you are left with is a raging destructive fire.

Marriage by definition is completely illogical. It seems totally absurd that two absolutely unique human beings could ever get together to build and share a life together. Marriage is doomed to fail unless it is rooted in God. Two become one only when they plug into the single all-embracing shared Universal Self.

Men and women, all people in fact, look at each other as though they are separate, but we are all totally connected to the same root and we are all getting our life force from the same source. We are like thousands of leaves on one tree—distinct and separate yet getting our sustenance from one root. We draw love for each other from the one divine wellspring. It has to be this way because we did not create love, we did not give it its value, and we did not instill within each other the need for love. It does not start with us and it does not end with us. Rather it flows through us when we are plugged in to the same divine circuitry of love. We enjoy eternal love when we meet at the deepest place of our beings; when we find our common source in the Great Universal I.

As we clarified previously, to connect to the divine, we must free ourselves from the trappings of persona and ego and embrace loneliness. When we do so, our relationships with other people are transformed. But if our soul is trapped in our persona and we think we are our egos, then we can relate only to the egos of others, and we never connect with their souls. Therefore, the Torah teaches, "Love your neighbor as *yourself,*" because if you cannot love your Self as a soul, you cannot love the self in someone else.

However, when the Torah says love your neighbor as yourself, it doesn't mean that you have to love your neighbor's ideas or opinions or actions. Indeed, you can hate his ideas, be annoyed by his talk and his walk, but still love his soul. We are commanded to love one another, and we can love one another because we are much more than just the characters we play. Each one of us is a soul, a ray of the Great Universal I. I am commanded to love your Self in the same way as I love my Self because we are both rays emanating from the one Great Self—God. Notice how that commandment in the Torah ends: "Love your neighbor as yourself, I am God." It is impossible not to love each other when we realize that we share in one Universal Self; that we are all expressions of God—the one and only Ultimate I.

The joy of true loving relationships only happens when we courageously face our existential loneliness and break through to our shared Universal Self. When all that we think, say, and do flows from our shared Self—the Great I—we experience daily life as nothing less than a constant celebration of divine love for ourselves, each other, and God.

Summary

Paradoxically, our individual Self discovers its connection with the Ultimate Self in profound moments of loneliness. When we fully embrace our inner incommunicable uniqueness and face our existential loneliness, we experience intimate communion with God and enjoy a loving companionship and partnership with him. Precisely when we hit the bedrock of our naked lonely existence, we mysteriously get the thrilling clarity that we are *never* alone because in the depth of feeling alone we encounter the All One. We understand that all the powers within us are not from us and therefore God is with us wherever we go. He is involved with us constantly—feeling our feelings, thinking our thoughts, and living our lives. Life becomes a loving partnership when we realize that God provides the raw substance of life—willpower, thoughts, feelings, mobility, etc.—but we must choose their form.

In every beat of our hearts we can hear God say, "I am with you. I love you. Be my partner in life."

Our loving relationship with God is also the foundation of all other loving relationships. The more we feel connected to God the more we feel connected to each other. The Torah instructs, "Love your neighbor as *yourself,* I am God." We are commanded to love each other in the same way we love our very own self because we are all like rays of light emanating from the One and Only Ultimate Self—God. Therefore, when we plug into the Soul of Souls—our shared Universal Self—we tap into the circuitry of all love.

As ecstatic as all this sounds there is yet another vital step that we must take to make I-contact and achieve true self-actualization. Once we freely transcend our egos and courageously face our existential loneliness we must then successfully integrate the conflicting drives of the two sides of our Self—the sacred and the creative.

4

The Creative Sacred Self

WE ALL HAVE ONLY ONE DESIRE in life and that is to be who we are. But who really are we? We are souls. But to each and every soul there are two sides—a sacred side and a creative side. These two sides of our souls impel us in seemingly opposing directions—outward and inward. When we properly address these apparently conflicting drives they become the source of tremendous creativity, productivity, stability, and fulfillment.

As we discussed in chapter 1, the Self (soul) is placed, so to speak, between the Me (persona) and the "I" (God). Because the soul is an expression of God—a ray of the Ultimate I—our sacred side yearns to retreat inward, relish the divine connection, and stay anchored in the Great Self. However the soul has also come to this world to serve a divine purpose, to play a role and do its part using its persona to channel God's presence on Earth. Therefore our creative side knows that we must master our persona. We must weave out of our God-given character strengths and weaknesses a wardrobe of psychological clothing that befits our godly greatness and accomplishes our earthly mission.

We live a push-pull. We are pushed out into the world to actualize our persona while pulled back to commune with the Great Self. Unless we make peace with our battle this push-pull phenomena will cause us great upheaval and torment. Properly navigating and balancing the conflicting dynamics of the soul is the secret to enormous creativity, productivity, inner peace, and ultimate fulfillment.

Two Sides, One Self

At the beginning of the Book of Genesis, we find two contradictory accounts of the creation of humanity that offer us a profound insight into the soul's paradoxical nature. Each of the two accounts portrays a different relationship between the first human being and God, and also between the first man and woman. We are going to examine these contradictions with the goal of understanding the contradiction we seem to be, and how we can reconcile our own opposing drives in order to accomplish our divine purpose and mission in life.

In the first account that the Book of Genesis offers, God decides to create a human being—called Adam after *adamah* ("Earth")—in his own image. He creates a man and a woman, commanding them to conquer the world and to use its natural resources to develop civilization:

> God said, "Let us make Adam in our image and likeness. Let him dominate the fish of the sea, the birds of the sky, the livestock animals, and all the earth, and every wild animal that walks the earth." God created Adam in His image. In the image of God, He created him, male and female He created them.[1]

In the second account the image of God is not mentioned, nor is anything said about dominating the Earth. Instead, we are told that God formed Adam from the dust of the earth and breathed into him his own breath—the "breath of life," or as some translate it, "a living soul." God then placed Adam in the Garden of Eden with the responsibility to take care of it.

> God formed Adam out of the dust of the ground and breathed into his nostrils a breath of life. Adam became a living creature. God planted a garden in Eden to the east. There He placed Adam whom He had formed. . . . God took

Adam and placed him in the Garden of Eden to work it and watch it.[2]

As in all stories recorded in the Torah, these differing nuances teach us profound lessons and have deep implications for our lives. Illuminating the traditional Jewish perspective, Rabbi Joseph B. Soloveitchik, a twentieth-century Torah scholar, explains in his book-long essay *The Lonely Man of Faith*[3] that, in these two different accounts, the Torah is describing the contradictory nature of man. Although at first glance it seems that the Torah is describing the creation of two completely different human beings, in fact, it is revealing the two faces of humanity. Rabbi Soloveitchik refers to these two expressions of ourselves as "Adam 1" and "Adam 2," both of whom are motivated by the same desire—to be who we are.

This is the basic drive of all people. We simply want to be ourselves. In fact, we tend to get annoyed with people who we feel are being phony. It's natural that everyone wants to be, and expects others to be, their true selves. But what really is the true self?

To each and every one of us there are two faces to our inner selves, but they are really two sides of one coin. If we understand and appreciate this fact, then these two sides that seem in conflict can instead become a source of tremendous life force.

Life in the Balance

Let's take a closer look at this dichotomy.

Adam 1 is a being created in the image of God, whom the Torah calls *Elohim,* a divine name used when referring to God as Creator. Since human beings are also described as created in the image of *Elohim* to be true to ourselves, we too want to be creators and accomplish mastery over our environment and thereby actualize our divine potential.

In fact, mastery is the mission statement of Adam 1. God charges humanity to conquer nature, develop it, and transform it. Not only is this our job, it is our quest. This is good, because by doing so, we are expressing our true self—the creative side of our soul—that was formed in the image of *Elohim*.

King David, praising God for the creation of man, wrote, "You made him a little lower than the angels and crowned him with honor and dignity."[4] In other words, God not only created us, but crowned us with the majestic ability to live an honorable and dignified life. Rabbi Soloveitchik explains that dignity is achieved through mastering our environment. A helpless brute, victimized by the natural forces surrounding him, does not live a dignified existence. We aspire to be majestic and dignified beings and, therefore, we must have mastery over our environment.

Since our mission as a creative soul is to live an honorable and dignified life, we must ask many "how" questions. When we look at nature we are intrigued by its power, and we try to figure out *how* to harness that power, *how* to take control of life, and *how* to overcome the limitations of time and space. Control and mastery are our measures of success.

Modern technology is one of the most significant expressions of the aspirations of our creative side. Success in technology means figuring out how to make things smaller, faster, and more manageable. Through technology, we are able to be aggressive and bold, determined to overcome the limitations of time and space and conquer the forces of the universe.

However, Adam 2—the sacred side of our soul—has a totally different interest in the universe and a different orientation to life. Our creative side seeks dignity and views nature's power, order, and beauty with an eye to harnessing and replicating it. Our sacred side, however, yearns for spiritual completion and seeks out the sublime, the holy, and the awesome. Instead of asking "how" questions, our sacred side leads us to "why" questions.

Our sacred side is interested in the philosophical and spiritual answer to questions such as: Why is this? What is this? Who is it? Where does all of this come from? Our sacred side is not concerned with the practical "how to."

As philosophers and spiritual seekers, we are not trying to conquer nature or develop the world. We are trying to understand it and establish an intimate relation with our Creator. Therefore, when the Torah metaphorically describes God as breathing into Adam 2 his own breath of life, an aspect of himself, it is alluding to the sacred side of us that is intimately preoccupied with God, yearning to experience personal communion with the source of our souls, the Soul of Souls, to feel complete and one with the Ultimate Self.

Whereas our creative side looks at the world from a quantitative point of view—how to measure it and thus control it—our sacred side looks for the qualitative, which cannot be measured scientifically. Our creative side, therefore, represents our scientific, technological, political, and artistic side, while our sacred side represents our philosophical, mystical, and religious yearnings. On the one hand, we seek to express our divine potential and emulate God's creativity and mastery over the universe; on the other hand, we yearn to retreat inward and feel our intimate identification with the Great Self and experience loving communion with God.

Because the world has become very developed on the creative side—technologically, scientifically, politically, and organizationally—we are now witnessing a great thirst to fulfill and express the sacred side of ourselves. This yearning is perhaps the basis of the New Age movement, which started in the 1970s and seeks to uncover the spiritual and the cosmic meaning of our existence.

As my editor and I were working on marketing an upcoming book of mine, I was concerned that the selling points were starting to sound too "New Age." But my editor explained that New Age had long ago gone mainstream. New Age–type people are no longer the only ones reading New Age books; everybody is reading them.

Clearly, we are seeing a spiritual renaissance happening today. The sacred aspect of humanity is coming more and more to the foreground of our consciousness.

Sacred Side on the Rise

It is unbelievable how technically advanced we have become. As my son and I were walking down the street in Jerusalem one day, he found it amazing that everyone around us was using a portable phone. His observation made me think: "We may be technically advanced, but are we spiritually advanced? Are we advanced in feeling the miracle and gift of life, in feeling connected to a greater reality? Are we advanced in our ability to celebrate daily the breathtaking mystery of simply being? Are we advanced in our power to live meaningfully and to love abundantly?"

These sacred concerns are becoming more and more prominent in our contemporary society. However, in the meantime, because of the extraordinary technological advancements, our creativity has progressed far ahead, while our spirituality has been left a bit behind. This imbalance, I believe, has nurtured a looming atmosphere of instability, insecurity, and anxiety.

Imagine you just spent $3,000 on a state-of-the-art computer, to realize only six months later that it's almost obsolete. You can't trade it in and you can't find replacement parts. Technology is advancing so fast that the stability and security that people thought they were going to get from technology is quickly turning into a source of tremendous insecurity. You just don't know what the value of your property will be tomorrow. You don't know whether the stock market will be up or down. It's very hard to know if what you just bought is really the latest, because the latest is already fading away; there is always something new and improved just over the horizon.

Many people put their faith in the future, hoping that the problems of life would be solved by technology. However, because more and more people are feeling that the future will bring instability, the past has become very attractive to the modern world. This is why when I wrote my first book *Endless Light,* my publisher persuaded me that its subtitle should be *The Ancient Path of the Kabbalah to Love, Growth, and Personal Power.* People want the "ancient path" because they figure that perhaps the ancients had something we don't have. We have computers and portable phones, but maybe they had the secret to spirit, happiness, and personal fulfillment; perhaps they were in touch with a higher self that empowered them to lead more meaningful and peaceful lives.

This growing concern points to the emergence of the sacred aspect of humanity. We are now asking existential questions, such as: "Who would I be if I lost everything I had? Who would I be if I lost my job and in the job market no one would take one look at me? Who would I be if I were paralyzed, God forbid, and all I could do was think? Would I be valuable? What legitimizes my existence? Is my existence valuable even if I cannot create and contribute to building this world? Is my sheer existence justified and worthwhile even if I just *am*? Even if I could do nothing more than just be?"

On the one hand, we feel valuable when we are productive and exerting mastery over our environment. On the other hand, we feel the need to acknowledge the existential value of simply being alive regardless of anything we can do or accomplish. The motto of our creative side is, "I work, therefore I am—and therefore I am valuable." But our sacred side is not satisfied with an existence where personal value depends upon what we do in relation to the outside world. Our sacred side boldly asserts, "God is, therefore I am—and therefore I am valuable." It informs us that our value will not be determined or measured by our accomplishments in the world but by the intrinsic worth of our soul as a part of God. Then we are truly a "someone"—some of the One. And to experience that truth we must celebrate our connection with God.[5]

Triumph in Defeat

The creative side of soul shines in victory. To make the most of our innate creativity we feel we must actualize our potential, employ our talents wisely, and become winners. We must conquer and triumph because we have to be in control. This is not a put-down of our creative side. These are the natural drives of that aspect of our soul that plays an earthly character, assumes a creative role, and is fulfilled, expressed, and realized. This is our God-given mandate, clear from the Book of Genesis, which tells us that we were formed in the image of the Creator. However, the sacred side of soul demands that we look for our existential value regardless of what we accomplish on Earth. We seek the worth of our inner self as connected to an ultimate reality, which we often discover only in times of defeat.

It is precisely when we fail and hit rock bottom that we start to ask existential questions about our inner self-worth. As long as we're at the top of the charts, progressing on the fast track, we are not likely to ask them.

I once met a CEO of one of the most successful movie companies in the world. As we were driving along in his Porsche, he pointed out the homes of the famous people living on his block. "I'm on a fast track," he said, "but I don't want to be on it too long. I want to go learn." I had no idea what he was talking about because in the Torah world when people say, "I want to learn," they generally mean they want to learn Torah. And he actually went on to say that that is what he wanted to do—he felt spiritually ready to go to Jerusalem. Like this movie mogul, most people know when they're on a fast track, but only some realize that the real winner is the one who knows when to get off before he gets pushed off the edge. The real winner will not wait for defeat to ask the big "why" questions about the meaning and value of existence.

This realization is what separates Adam 1 and Adam 2—our creative side and our sacred side—when the going gets tough. Our creative side shines in times of victory and success, while our sacred side shines in times of defeat and failure. It is precisely when we lose everything, when we feel abandoned and alone that we are forced to ask who we really are and what life's challenges really mean. In overcoming addictions to work, money, sex, drugs and alcohol, we realize that we need to include some element of surrender in our lives to improve ourselves. This mindset reflects the success of the popular twelve-step program that has taken the world by storm. The first step is to accept that there is a higher power and acknowledge that we cannot solve our problems on our own. Ironically, surrender to God is empowering.

The spiritual quest of our sacred side often begins when crisis sets in. Our sacred side often emerges from deep within when we experience the death of a loved one, go through a divorce, lose our money, or helplessly watch our children get involved in drugs or cults. Although it doesn't have to work this way, it is nevertheless common that when people fail, they allow the sacred side of their soul to finally seek God. This is what King David meant when he wrote, "Out of the depths, I call to You, O God."[6] People seek God in times of trouble. Our sacred side often begins to flourish precisely in difficult times and defeat, when our lives feel like they are coming apart. Only then are we driven to look beyond ourselves—in a genuine attempt to evaluate *why* we want to win, what we want to win, and what is the meaning and value of our lives independent of any external accomplishments.

I once met a very wealthy man who flew all over the world in his private jet to meet with top international business executives. I said to him, "Wow, that is exciting. How do you feel?" He answered, "I feel lonely. I know that if I were to lose my money, no one would give me the time of day." I was shocked and saddened that this powerful, highly successful man lives with this terrible, lowly feeling. Our self-worth, in terms of the creative side of our soul, is completely dependent on the success of our persona; our Me. And for many of us it is expressed in completely superficial and insignificant terms. It is about the money, power, and fame that we amass and not about how we use our basic character traits to do good and serve on Earth. But in terms of the sacred side of our soul, we know that our value is based on something else—our essence as an aspect of God.

The quest of our creative side is dignity as achieved through creativity, productivity, and mastery. The sacred side of our soul, however, is looking for something more: it is looking for completion and wholeness—a feeling of personal adequacy and inner worth that is not dependent on achievement.

We wonder: "Does it make sense that someone should help me, even though I cannot help them in return? Will people be nice to me only if I can reciprocate? Is life always a business deal? Can I be loved because I am a soul, a part of God, regardless of what a person can get from me?"

Once, following a class I taught about this idea, a student came to my office crying. She had never felt that anybody would be nice to her unless she deserved it and somehow justified her legitimate right to it. She had never experienced pure unconditional love. It was a remarkable idea to her that just because we exist, we are valuable.

This idea shook her foundation because as someone who was totally into her creative side, she did not really understand kindness. Looking at the world from the point of view of dominance and mastery, she felt that people were kind to her only because they expected her to be kind to them. But this is not really kindness. This is business. But from the point of view of the soul's sacred side, kindness is a natural aspect of who we are as a part of God—we are nice to others for no reason and with no expectation of anything in return.

Kindness was one of Abraham's great contributions to the world. Abraham was the epitome of kindness. He had a tent that had no walls—it was just a roof—so that he could have maximum visibility of any stranger in the vicinity and invite him to dinner.

The Midrash relates that when Abraham's guests would thank him for his hospitality, Abraham would simply say, "Don't thank me. Thank the Master of the World." If the guests weren't willing to thank God, Abraham would say, "Then pay me." When I first read this Midrash, I found it very strange. It sounds like some evangelistic plot to bring people to God-consciousness by being nice to them, but only in return for their payment with faith.

Abraham, in fact, was brilliant. What he was really saying was this: "If you really don't believe in God, why would you think that I would do anything nice for you without any expectation of payment in return? Realize that you are valuable to me because there is a God and you are and I are expressions of one ultimate and shared Divine Self. Therefore, I love you and care about you regardless of what you do, without any expectation of anything in return. I love you simply because you are. Love and care flow naturally from my heart to you because I am a part of God and so are you. If we exist, then we are divinely valuable and should be treated in a divinely valued way. Each and every one of us is a masterpiece—a piece of the Master—and surely deserves to be treated that way."

Summary

To each and every one of us there are two aspects of ourselves—the sacred and the creative—but they are really two sides of one coin and together express the soul's one desire. We simply want to be who we are. But who are we? On one hand we are expressions of God—rays of the Great Self. But on the other hand, we have been given a character and role to play in this physical world. God has gifted us with character traits, strengths, and weaknesses that are meant to be used in service of the divine purpose on Earth.

Our sacred side yearns to retreat inward, transcend our earthly character and remain anchored in the Great Self. It simply wants to forever delight in our intimate connection to God. But our creative side knows that we must go out and advance forward on a quest for success in actualizing our potential on Earth. We live a push-pull. We are pushed out into the world to master and actualize our persona (Me) while pulled back to commune with our Ultimate I. When we understand and appreciate this fact, these apparently conflicting drives become the very source of enormous creativity, productivity, stability, and fulfillment. A necessary step toward making I-contact—self-actualization and fulfillment—is balancing and integrating our creative and sacred sides. We must master the dynamics of our persona—our strengths and weaknesses, talents and flaws, social status and challenges—to successfully accomplish our creative mission on Earth, but for God's sake—rooted in the Ultimate I in humble service of God's purpose. The payoff is integrity—a powerful synergy of dignified living and spiritual completeness rooted in unconditional self-worth and love.

5

Integrity, Unconditional Self-Worth, and Love

W E EXPERIENCE DIGNITY when we actualize our creative side by going out into the world, mastering and developing it using the unique talents and traits of our persona—our Me. We enjoy spiritual completion when we actualize our sacred side by retreating inward, conquering ourselves, communing with and surrendering to our Ultimate I—God. Self-actualization happens when we balance and synergize our drive for personal dignity and our thirst for spiritual completion. The goal is integrity—to become both a powerful master and a humble servant. We need to develop our personas and skillfully use our talents but with the humble intent of serving to bring God's love and goodness to others, infusing the world with Divine Presence. To do this we must know when to assert and control—when to be bold, courageous and aggressive—and when to give up control and surrender to God.

We may think we are independent, but the truth is that we are always serving something or someone. But there is tremendous joy in serving God's purpose because in doing so we go beyond our narrow selves and discover ourselves as part of an ultimate reality beyond us. We experience our connection to our Ultimate Self when we live as a channel for God's love and goodness.

The Midrash says that a humble servant of a king has the status of a king—just like when you come close to fire, you too become warm. Therefore, the more you live your connection to God, the more godliness you radiate and the more godly you feel. This is the ultimate union of dignity and spiritual completion.

Gratefully Unaccomplished

You can meet people who live a very dignified lifestyle—they have beautiful grounds, stately homes with magnificent interior design complete with priceless art, and an incredible ability to manage international corporations. They are highly skilled, efficient, competent, and confident in what they do. These people enjoy an honorable and majestic life. They have reached the top of the ladder in dignity, but they are spiritually unaware and incomplete. How is that so? Being dignified is unlike being spiritually complete. Completion is an awareness of the divine nature of being. It's about getting in touch with the miraculous truth of simply being, regardless of accomplishing anything or impressing anyone.

Once when I was sitting in a park, I was feeling very grateful for the many wonderful things in my life—my family, health, talents, career, home, and so on. I wondered, what did I do to deserve any of this? Can I say that I have children because I did something right and, therefore, deserved to be entrusted with human life? As I sat and realized that I did nothing to deserve the blessings in my life, I then thought, what *could* I have done to deserve them? How much good would I have to do to earn children? How many great deeds in my life would it take to earn a kidney, heart, brain, or any other part of my body? I couldn't come up with an answer. Life—and all it includes—is priceless.

Think about it—for what amount of money would you be willing to sell your arm? If someone said to you, "Listen, buddy, I'd like to buy your arm. I'll give you five million dollars for it," would you take it? How about twenty million dollars for one eye? Even for all that money, I still wouldn't do it. In fact, I don't know who would. Even if a person had the noble intention of giving the money to charity, it still would be wrong. We have no right to sell our children, our arms, or our eyes because they don't belong to us. They belong to God.

Once I realized how remarkable life is and that I did nothing to deserve any of my blessings, I felt a little guilty. But then it hit me—life is simply a gift. I should just humbly and gratefully accept it. This is the beginning of realizing and appreciating the intrinsic divine value of being and feeling spiritually complete.

The Book of Lamentations, the account of Jeremiah's anguish over the destruction of the Temple, makes a statement that underscores the value of human life. At the time it was written, the world seemed as though it were being destroyed. Thousands of Jews were exiled and murdered, and blood was flowing in the streets of Jerusalem. Amid all the pain and destruction, Jeremiah wrote: "What does a living man have to complain about?"

In other words, just being alive should be enough for us to be thankful and not complain. While this realization is very deep and not easy to integrate, the important thing is to develop an awareness of the pure divine nature and incredible value of just being.

To Have or to Be

Spiritual completion, in contrast to dignity (which is dependent on mastery and accomplishment), is not just an extraneous or incidental attribute among other attributes of being. Completion is a mode of being in itself. It is not about what you have or what you have accomplished; it is about who you are. It is not about *having* but *being*. What you have you can lose, but who you are nobody can take away from you.

I actually learned this concept from my son when he was four years old. One evening, as we sat together for story-telling time, he told me, "Daddy, there was a ship in the sea and it was attacked by pirates. They robbed the entire ship and took everything from everybody. But there was one man on the ship who didn't lose anything."

"Who was that?" I asked him.

"It was the religious man," he said, wide-eyed.

"Why didn't he lose anything?" I asked, on the edge of my seat.

"Because what he had they couldn't take away from him."

"What was that?"

"Torah," he said. "Daddy, if you have Torah, no one can take that away from you."

I was very impressed. When I was four years old, Humpty Dumpty was the deepest sample of my story-telling repertoire.

Why can't Torah be taken away from you? Because Torah is not something you have. Torah is something you become. Torah is not a collection of wisdom that you own. It is vehicle of transformation—from simple being to being holy.

The prophetic wisdom and guidance of Torah is meant to empower us to take control of ourselves, bringing self-respect, godly order, and discipline into our lives by identifying ourselves with the Great I, God. Torah enables us to get in touch with the unconditional intrinsic worth of our soul in communion with our Ultimate Self, God.

Therefore, spiritual completion is not about acquiring techniques for conquering our environment, but conquering ourselves. It is a celebration of who we really are as a part of God.

A spiritually complete existence is intrinsically different than an incomplete existence. One man may be a well-known public figure living the life of luxury in a mansion and another man might be an unknown living a poor life in a shack, but intrinsically these two people may be very much the same. In fact, the man in the shack may be spiritually complete, his soul shining out with incredible inner divine worth, while the man in the mansion may suffer severe low self-esteem.

I once heard an interview with the singer-actress, Cher, that illustrates this point well. She was talking about how she felt about herself, and she said, "I've always had low self-esteem." She went on to explain, "Well, most people in this industry have low self-esteem. Why else would we be out here on stage, in the spotlight, looking for acknowledgment?"

Cher is right. Receiving acknowledgement from applause and having your name in bright lights does not empower you to find your inner divine light. Despite the fact that Cher is successful, accomplished, beautiful, talented, and, I am sure, a very confident performer, she still suffers from low self-esteem. Accomplishment might give her honor and dignity, but it does not satisfy her hunger for spiritual completion and unconditional self-worth.

Many people enjoy a status of dignity—money, power, prestige. They are honorable and well-known personalities and yet their lives are spiritually incomplete; they have no inner security. They suffer daily anxiety and a constant fear that they may any day lose all of their external trappings. They cannot stop working and just relax to take some sacred time for just *being*.

Having worthwhile assets doesn't necessarily make us feel that we are worthwhile. Having power and control of the world outside of us doesn't help us feel the true divine essence and eternal value of our soul.

Now don't get me wrong—I am not saying that there is something wrong with wealth or power. Wealth and power can be expressions of our creative side but we will never feel whole without actualizing our sacred side. We are meant to conquer the world, but as a soul, as a part of God in service of a godly purpose.

Spiritual completion does not have to be acted out in the world. You don't need to act upon something or someone else to help you feel complete. You don't need to tell somebody else, and you don't need somebody else to tell you, that you are complete. If you need somebody else to tell you this, then you are not complete, your self-worth is conditional. It depends on getting enough approval and acknowledgement. And it is never enough. A hermit, attuned to his soul connection to God, is more spiritually complete than even a king who reigns supreme but neglects nurturing the awareness of his eternal connection to God. Such a hermit delights in unconditional divine self-worth while the king who looks good on the outside may feel bad about himself on the inside.

Spiritual completion is something you can only come to know from inside yourself by virtue of your internal and eternal connection with God. Of course, what we do outside can help us access and affirm this realization inside. But the truth of your spiritual completion and true self-worth lies within.

Dignity, on the other hand, is acted out in the world. It sounds something like this: "I am talented, competent, and confident . . . I conquered nature . . . I am technologically savvy . . . I built a successful business . . . People acknowledge and honor me."

Success in the outside world is the way to dignity, but spiritual completion is rooted in the conquest of your inner world. Your inner unconditional self-worth comes from communing with the Great Self. It is a deep power and relentless sense of security derived from being anchored in God; knowing and affirming that we are each an expression of God.

Completion is found in the privacy of one's own in-depth soul experience. We experience it as a catharsis, a truth that is released from within. It cannot be drawn from any outside source; rather, it can only be accessed from within by tapping into our innermost self as it connects to the Self of all selves. When we dig deep inside we will surely find the gold within, or more specifically, the God within.

Becoming Complete through Defeat

While dignity is accomplished when we boldly advance forward and confront the outside world, spiritual completion is attained when we advance inward to confront ourselves. To be dignified we must have mastery over our environment, business, money, property, and so on. But to be spiritually complete we must have mastery over ourselves. And while dignity is triumphantly conquering the forces of nature, completion is about conquering ourselves and humbly allowing ourselves to be confronted and defeated by a higher power—God.

Dignity is discovered at the peak of success but completion often happens at the depths of crisis and failure. When you are overpowered by God, surrender to his will and completely give yourself over to him.

Ironically defeat is often our greatest triumph. Defeat in the arena of the outside world can bring us to great inner victory and spiritual completion. We as souls come out as winners when we courageously face defeat and wholeheartedly affirm our 100 percent unconditional self-worth. Regardless of how bitterly we may fail in worldly accomplishments or in our public image we must always remember that we are created in a divine image. We are souls, rays of God; nothing and no one can take that away unless we give it away.

In other words, completion comes from learning to let go and let God. There is great joy in surrendering and trusting that we can't always get what we want and we can't always have it our way. We can let go and be at peace because we know that our self-worth is unconditional. It does not depend on getting what we want or having it our way. Spiritually complete people know that they are not the director of the show. People who defiantly insist, "It's my life!" have it wrong. They are selling themselves short. This kind of thinking completely undermines the value of life. As we discussed earlier, it's not our life—it's really God's. The life that we think we own we really owe to God. Our life is only on loan. When we sense this truth, we are able to trust that things are going to work out; we let go and trust in God. Of course God is taking care of us. Whatever happens is always in our best interest because God loves us unconditionally. He loves us with the same love he has for his very own self because indeed we are a part of him.

The Talmud says if a person loses his temper, it's as if he is worshipping idols. How can that be? We see people lose their temper all the time, yet they are hardly pagans.

People lose their tempers because things do not go according to their plans. They are unwilling to trust in and surrender to a higher power and demand to be completely in control of their lives—as if they are gods. They worship themselves and their own plans.

To trust God means to accept that life always goes according to God's plans. In fact, participating in a higher divine plan is really what gives our lives the greatest value. We then experience ourselves as actors in an eternal divine drama and not just some petty little self-produced play that is here today and gone tomorrow. Life is a mere fleeting moment when it's just your story or mine. But when it's a part of God's Story it's simply divine. We are blessed with a spiritual completion when we trust in and surrender to God's higher plan, move out of the limelight, and humbly seek to serve.

We must take control when we climb the ladder of dignity, but for spiritual completion we must know when to let go. We must give up the reins and realize that we are not the reigning power. Oddly enough surrender is the secret to unconditional self-worth and empowerment. It is also the secret to accomplishing unconditional love.

Unconditional Love

Intimate loving relationships often fail because we are dominated by our creative side's desire for dignity. We therefore seek a mate only in order to pool our talents together for success. Our sacred side, however, wants love to be spiritually complete. We yearn for intimate companionship, not just productive partnership. Whereas our creative side looks for someone we can *work* with, our sacred side seeks someone we can *be* with—to share tears, laughter, and the ineffable wonder of being at all.

In the first biblical account of creation the first human being is androgynous, created as both man and woman:

> God created man in His own image, in the image of God He created him; male and female He created them.[1]

In the second account, the man is created first. He is lonely, but cannot find a suitable mate among the animals, and so God removes a part of him and makes a woman.

And the Lord God sent a deep sleep on the man, and took one of the bones from his side while he was sleeping, joining up the flesh again in its place: And the bone which the Lord God had taken from the man he made into a woman, and took her to the man. The man said, "This is now bone of my bones, and flesh of my flesh; She shall be called Woman, because she was taken out of Man."[2]

In the first account Adam did not have to make a sacrifice in order for his female partner to come into his life. Together they were to conquer the world and actualize themselves as they were formed to be in the image of Creator. In the second account, however, Adam had to give away part of himself in order to meet his companion, teaching us that to really find your soul mate, you have to give yourself over.

We often fail at creating intimate loving relationships because we are dominated by our creative side. Remember, our creative side in search of godly dignity is success-minded. We therefore enter into relationships because we understand that two heads are better than one. We are like a clever entrepreneur who knows that pooling talents and resources together increases our chances of succeeding in our conquest of the Earth. We stay together only as long as we win together and benefit each other to reach our goals. Of course, this is not love—this is business. Together we may achieve dignity but not spiritual completion.

To achieve true love and intimacy we need to nurture our sacred side. We must turn our attention toward living a complete relationship. To feel completion in a relationship we need to feel, for instance, that we don't have to do anything special for our mate in order to earn his or her love. We can expect to be loved just because we are soul mates. If you were to ask your spouse, "Why do you love me?" you would want to hear, "No reason; just because you're you." If there is a reason, it's not love; the other person loves the reason, not you. And you will then wonder what will happen if that reason ceased to be.

When you reach this level of loving your spouse because he or she exists, then no matter what challenges arise in your life, the relationship will survive. A relationship that is built on mutual love rather than on mutual benefit cannot be destroyed.

In the Garden of Eden, before God created Eve, Adam was given the task of assigning names to the animals in order to pinpoint his soul mate. When he looked at all the animals, he realized that he could not share himself with them. Perhaps functionally they could work together, benefit each other, harness their powers together, and be productive, but he could not share his inner self with them and just be together. Animals don't experience true love and intimacy because they cannot experience loneliness. Loneliness happens when you get in touch with your singular unique Self and ask those existential questions like "Who am I? Why am I?" Animals do not ask these kinds of questions. They don't have identity crises when they lose their favorite bone.

But because of his sacred side, Adam asked himself, "Who am I, and what is my inner worth?" And thus he was not compatible with any animal. Our sacred side looks for intimate companionship, not just productive partnership. Perhaps Adam's creative side would have been satisfied with finding another creature with whom he could mate, reproduce himself, and build a work force. Adam's sacred side, however, looked for a mate with whom he could share himself and communicate. He did not look for someone he could *work* with but someone he could *be* with.

Have you ever looked into the eyes of an animal as opposed to someone you love? There is a difference! You may be able to see "eye to eye," but you are not able to connect "I to I." When two lovers stare into each other's eyes, they enjoy an inner connection that is incommunicable. Eyes are windows to the soul. In that intimate exchange, lovers enjoy profound fulfillment in the here and now even though there is no measurable accomplishment.

God said, "It is not good for man to be alone." But Adam wasn't really alone; there were plenty of animals in the Garden of Eden to play with. The verse in the Torah actually reads, "It is not good that the man is lonely." When we're looking for spiritual completion, we have to address our loneliness. We may never be alone—having plenty of colleagues to work with in the office, going to many business meetings during the day and parties at night and so forth. And yet we may feel profoundly lonely because we're missing true companionship, someone to share our incommunicable inner self; someone to celebrate the ineffable miracle of simply being at all.

This is why Adam was lonely despite being surrounded by animals. Adam felt separate from his environment because he had no one with whom to commune. Even the first woman, who according to the first biblical account was created simultaneously with Adam for the purpose of working together to conquer the nature, would not have solved the loneliness rooted in Adam's sacred side. For Adam to find his soul mate and experience completion, he had to first experience his existential loneliness. He had to realize that, although he was not alone, he was lonely. After meeting and naming all the animals, Adam discovered his own uniqueness and painfully recognized just how exclusive and lonely he really was. When he fully understood his incompatibility with any other being he must have felt greatly defeated and yet this defeat was truly the basis of success.

As we discussed earlier, loneliness is the necessary foundation of true love and intimacy. Defeated, Adam was left with a profound yearning for intimacy with a companion who was as unique as he was. He longed for someone with whom he could share his inner self; someone to share the tears, share the laughter, and share the extraordinary wonder of being.

To create intimacy, you have to give a part of yourself to somebody else. For this reason, before God created Eve, he made an overpowering sleep fall upon Adam and created Eve out of him. To find a business partner, you have to be success minded and willing to share your talents and resources, put your heads together, and get to work to accomplish your mutual goals. But to find your soul mate, you must be willing to feel defeated and lonely and be able to surrender and give yourself over to another. You must be able to accept love even when you feel like a loser and be loved for the sheer sake of being, unrelated to any accomplishments or anything you can offer in return. Only then can you love another and be loved by another unconditionally. Our sacred side knows, "Even when I am incapable of doing anything productive, I exist as a part of God, and therefore I am valuable and loveable."

We actualize our creative side and connect with others to ensure a better future for ourselves. We can then conquer more and achieve greater productivity and success. But our sacred side seeks to connect with others for no other reason than to share intimacy and be together—here and now.

God wants us to be whole; to embrace and integrate our creative and sacred sides. He created us with these two aspects that together reveal the divinity of our true selves—our creative sacred soul—in order to bridge heaven and Earth and serve to channel his goodness into the world.

Summary

Dignity is mastery over our environment using the unique traits of our persona—our Me. It is discovered at the peak of success. Spiritual completion, however, often happens at the depths of crisis and failure. It is mastery over our inner self, communing with and surrendering to the Great Self—God. It is a profound feeling of unconditional self-worth stemming from the fact that our individual Self is anchored in the Greater Universal Self.

Intimate loving relationships often fail because we are dominated by our creative side's desire for dignity. We therefore seek a mate only in order to pool our talents together for success. Our sacred side, however, wants love to be spiritually complete. We yearn for intimate companionship, not just productivity; we want a soul mate, not a business partner.

Our ultimate goal, however, is to embrace our creative and sacred side, integrate personal dignity with spiritual completion, and become both a powerful master and a humble servant of God's purpose. We are then whole and spiritually healthy, living and celebrating our godly greatness and relentlessly actualizing our divine potential. We must, however, always remember that the inner greatness that drives us is not ours. And we need to deeply understand why on Earth are we here.

6

Big Ego or Great Soul

IT IS SAD but true that much of the world today is plagued
with low self-esteem and chronic self-deprecation. People
simply don't believe in themselves. We are spiritually healthy
when we know from deep inside that we are radiant, powerful,
significant, and great. If this is not obvious then we are seriously
disconnected from ourselves and God. How could we think of
ourselves as anything less than awesome if we knew that our soul
was none other than an aspect and expression of God—the Great
Self. Spiritually healthy people intuit their godly greatness from
within and are constantly driven to actualize their divine potential by doing great acts for their community, the world, and God.

Self-actualization is often misunderstood to mean that I actualize Me—I become fully me, I use my talents to their utmost and
successfully define and assert my individuality. My personal fulfillment does not necessarily have anything to do with anybody
else. This understanding of self-actualization does not include
any sense of national responsibility or commitment to God. But,
in truth, there is no such thing as an individual soul existing independent and apart from a collective national soul or the Universal
Soul.

Kabbalah teaches that we are not isolated beings floating in
outer space, disconnected from a greater context. Each individual
soul is really an individualistic expression of the national soul of
his or her people, which itself is an aspect of the Universal Soul,
the Soul of souls, God. We find personal meaning and fulfillment

only to the extent that we contribute in our own unique way to the betterment of our nation, the world, and the fulfillment of God's purpose.

Kabbalah teaches that a nation is not simply the sum total of many individuals. Rather, a nation is a whole that is greater than the sum of its parts. In fact, each soul is a unique expression of the whole nation, born out of the collective soul of the nation. Therefore, even though each of us is an individual, we are personally meaningful only because we are members of our nation's soul—shareholders in its national destiny.

In addition, just as an individual soul has a body, so too the national soul has a body. The body of a nation is its land. The body of the collective soul of the American people is comprised of the fifty states of United States of America. The body of the collective soul of the British people is the island of Great Britain. The body of the collective soul of the Jewish people is the Land of Israel.

I think this is one of the common epiphanies for many Jews when they visit Israel—the Promised Land. I recall the first time I toured the borders of Israel and heard heroic stories about young Israeli soldiers who valiantly defended their country from invading armies and sacrificed their lives for the Jewish people. These selfless soldiers gave up their individual lives so that their nation could live on. I wondered then: "Is there such a reality called national life? Does a nation have a collective soul that encompasses the individual souls of its constituents?"

Kabbalah also teaches that the national soul is a unique expression of the Universal Soul, the Soul of souls—God. Therefore, an individual soul is also an individualistic expression of the Universal Soul. This further explains the meaning of the belief that each of us is created in the image of God. Each of us is an exclusive irreplaceable expression of God. God becomes manifest through the unique vantage points of every nation and every individual soul. Therefore, there is no such thing as an individual soul that exists separate and independent of its nation's soul and of the Universal Soul. And true self-actualization can only be accomplished when we are concerned with contributing to the actualization of our nation's destiny, helping to improve the world and serving to make manifest God's goodness and love on Earth.

For example, if I, David Aaron, perceive myself as an independent entity, existing apart and separate from the Jewish people, humanity, and God then I am actually alienating myself from my true self. My true self is an individual expression of the collective soul of the Jewish people, the world, and God. Therefore, when I neglect the needs of my people, the needs of the world, and the will of God, I neglect myself. If I really cared about myself, then I would really care about my people, humanity, and God. Therefore, selflessly serving your community, the world, and God is the only true way to self-actualization. To be selfless is truly selfish— to be selfish is to lose yourself.

The Holy Side of Pride

The Torah teaches that not one of our character traits is absolutely negative; everything has a role. All we have to do is look at each trait with an open mind and determine its pluses and the minuses.

When it comes to pride we must always take care to probe our inner psyche and determine whether the prideful thoughts and feelings we have about ourselves are coming from egotistical illusions of existing independent of the community and God or from our soul as an expression of a Greater Self. When prideful thoughts come from our ego then they are self-destructive. They alienate us from our true self as it expresses and interfaces with our national self, international self, and the Ultimate Self, God. But when these feelings of great self-worth come from our soul then they are precious and self-affirming. They verify our connection to the collective soul of our people, the world, and the Universal Soul. This sense of pride confirms that our true self is an expression of the power and beauty of our people, humanity, and God.

Scientifically, we are not even one-billionth of a speck of dust relative to the universe. How, then, is it possible that anybody could ever think that their existence is significant? And yet, not only do people think they are really something, some even think they are everything, the be-all-and-end-all of existence. Where would they get such a ridiculous idea? They could get it from their soul, which is a unique manifestation of the be-all-and-end-all, God. But it may be the wild conjuring of their ego.

When prideful thoughts and feelings erupt within us, we should not deny them and quickly put them down. We must clarify whether they are coming from our soul or from our ego. Sometimes our prideful thoughts are really an expression of the true grandeur of our soul as an expression of the eternal grandeur of God. In that case we must, nonetheless, be careful that our ego does not take these precious prideful thoughts and feelings and use them to lead us away from their true source and meaning. We must always remind ourselves that the grandeur we sense from within is not *our* greatness but God's. Otherwise our ego will use these powerful feelings of high self-esteem and confuse us into thinking that this greatness comes from us, independently of anyone beyond us. The ego often appropriates these holy sparks of divine self-worth causing us much damage, alienating us from our true self rooted in the collective soul of our people, humanity, and God.

Being Good versus Looking Good

How can you know when prideful thoughts are coming from egotistical delusions versus the truth of the soul?

I once shared with a friend my passion to reach people worldwide and help them improve the spiritual quality of their lives. I asked him, "But where is all this coming from? Is it a profound inner sense of my calling and destiny? Is God speaking to me through the restless stirrings of my soul that this is my divine service? Or perhaps this is just my self-serving ego seeking the limelight. How can I know if it's my ego or my soul driving me?"

My friend answered me, "If you use your drives to do good, help people, and improve the world, then it is the holiest self-service you could do. It will then obviously be your soul. But if you use your drives just to gain acknowledgement and become famous, it will be your ego. Ultimately you will decide."

In other words, there is nothing wrong with feeling proud and thinking you are special, powerful, and talented, as long as you use all that to do great things for others and God. Only when you feel good about yourself will you do good for others, and only when you do good for others will you truly feel good about yourself. Is your drive for success derived from the greatness of your soul as an expression of a higher more inclusive self? Is it coming from a sense of your spiritual mission and desire to serve your people, humanity, and God? Or is it just ego? It simply depends on whether you desire to *be* good or simply *look* good.

Sometimes people undermine the good that they could do by assuming that humility demands they step out of the limelight. However, there is nothing wrong with confidently acknowledging your talents and strengths; on the contrary, there is something very wrong when you *don't* acknowledge them. If, for example, you have a talent for public speaking, then your "gift of gab" is a gift from God and you have a responsibility to your people, humanity, and God to use it. If you don't use your God-given talents then you are an ingrate. In fact, not using your talents is a sign that you really think these talents are yours and not God's. This attitude is actually a very subtle form of a big ego.

On the other hand, it would be self-destructive if you forgot that your talents are God-given gifts and mistakenly think of them as coming from your strength, your power. This kind of pride only alienates you from God as the true source of your strengths and the divine purpose of your talents (to serve your people, the world, and God by materializing spiritual divine values and ideals on Earth).

If you reject the holy self-esteem that stirs within you, you will not only fail to achieve any good for yourself and others, but you will eventually become depressed and angry. You are stifling, and ultimately strangling, your soul. If you have been given the ability to be a brilliant businessman, a skilled surgeon, or an awesome composer, and you hide your light because you think being humble is a more godly trait, then you are seriously confused. You need to understand the difference between the ego, which separates you from God, and the true sense of mission, which requires you to humbly serve God with all the resources he has blessed you with. The Torah teaches: "You shall love the Lord, your God with all your heart, with all your soul, and with all your might."[1]

Truly humble people recognize that their *might*—talents and strengths—are God-given and they are incredibly passionate about using them to serve their people, humanity, and God. Those who are not truly humble are allowing their egos to rule them, albeit clad in a garb of false humility. This false humility will eventually cause them to become angry and depressed because they are not allowing their soul to shine through the unique and God-given garb of their persona. Some people actually fool themselves into thinking that this kind of self-deprecating humility is an expression of their closeness to God. They may think "I am so close to God because I diminish myself and avoid taking center stage." But their attitude actually expresses their alienation from God and a rejection of his gifts and their responsibility to use them.

God wants to make manifest through us his wisdom, creativity, kindness, justice, compassion, peace, and beauty to improve the world. (We will learn more how this works according to Kabbalah in chapter 7.) We must learn to draw our drive and determination from the grandeur of God seeking to become present in the world through you and me. We must get our egos out of the way and let our souls radiate God's light!

Let the Real You Shine

A true believer in God naturally believes in himself. And a true believer in himself naturally believes in God. True faith is empowering. Egomaniacs believe in themselves but only in themselves. Truly humble people, however, believe in themselves because they are a part of God. They know that God believes in them and seeks to become manifest through them to bring his goodness into the world. Truly humble people know that as a soul they are an expression of God, and therefore they could not be anything less than great and forever worthwhile.

Rabbi Nachman of Breslov, the great eighteeth-century Hassidic master, taught that people have to be careful to always see the good in themselves. If you ever feel overwhelmed with low self-esteem, flooded with doubts about your self-worth, then relentlessly remind yourself that you are a soul, nothing less than a part of God. This is an eternal fact and there is nothing that you can do that could ever damage that truth. No matter what you do, no matter how low you go, your inner self is pure divine light. Your wrongdoings cannot change that truth but they can conceal that truth. Take pride in the fact that you are a soul and know that you are definitely holy. Constantly encourage yourself to act in ways that will express the truth of your inner godly greatness. Chant to yourself over and over again: "I am a soul, I am holy, I am good and I owe it to myself, my people, the world, and God to act holy, do good, and affirm who I really am."

You may have assumed a negative persona. But that only means that your psychological clothing is dirty—*you* are not dirty. Your dirty clothing makes you look dirty and feel dirty, but you are clean. So wash your clothing, clean up your act, and you will feel and reveal the pure beautiful divine you. Your true essential self is holy and good, and you must remind yourself of that truth. Do something good, even something small, and you will feel great because that good deed is a peephole into the real you. God, the Great I, is waiting to be revealed through you, so what are you waiting for? Do good and let God's light shine through you.

The great mystic and philosopher of the twentieth century, Rabbi Abraham Isaac Kook, taught that we must see the good aspects even in our faults and deficiencies. What could be the good aspects in all our faults? Part of the daily Jewish liturgy is a blessing that states, "Blessed are You, God, who has created all my needs." Rabbi Kook explains that everything you have is exactly what you need to grow and succeed in your mission on Earth. As we discussed earlier not only are your strengths and positive characteristics necessary but also your weaknesses and negative character traits. These are God-given problems and challenges.

Some people are born with a tendency to be lazy, others with an inclination to be disorganized. Some have an explosive passion for sex and others may be wildly driven to amass money and power. We all have challenges, but we have to understand how important these challenges are; how vital they are to our very existence here on Earth. Our problems, flaws, and negative inclinations are really divine opportunities in the obstacle course of life. They offer us the ability to work harder and jump higher.

Recently, a student at Isralight confided in me that she was suffering from low self-esteem; she said that she simply didn't like herself. She found that during the field trips nobody wanted to sit next to her on the bus. This confirmed that indeed she was not well liked. I asked my wife, Chana, for her thoughts about how people can overcome low self-esteem, and she made a very important point. She suggested that maybe dealing with low self-esteem is not about finding a solution to overcome it, but about learning how to use it as a propulsion force.

Very often the most successful people actually suffer low self-esteem. In fact, it is precisely their low self-esteem that has driven them to the top. In their attempt to overcome their low self-esteem, they have pushed forward and made major contributions to this world. If a person, in an attempt to feel good about herself, does good in the world then she has actually turned her problem into a gift to herself and the world; she has turned it into a service of God to manifest goodness in the world. Every character trait can be used for good. You decide for yourself what to do with it.

In our daily prayers we empower ourselves to grow by recognizing that everything we have in our lives—the positive and the negative—is exactly what we need to fulfill our mission in life. Is it realistic to think that we can completely rid ourselves of the feelings of low self-esteem? No. Some of it goes all the way back to childhood, and it is very entrenched. Some of us are still dealing with what our teacher or friend said to us in kindergarten. Perhaps the answer is to accept our low self-esteem as a daily problem that will never to be completely overcome. Without it, we might stop feeling compelled to improve ourselves. Maybe the purpose of our low self-esteem is to present us with the challenge to work harder at feeling better about ourselves by affirming our godly self; doing good in the world for the sake of humanity and God.

When you look at your low self-esteem in this way, you will not feel depressed and defeated by it but rather thankful for it. You will see it as a catalyst for growth. Once you resolve to seek the divine good in all your faults and weaknesses, these problems are at once turned into godly gold.

If it is your nature to be stingy, but you want to be generous, then every time you overcome your stingy character—even for only a moment—and act in a kindly way, then your act of kindness is greater than that of a person who is naturally inclined to be kind. If it is your nature to be sad, but you want to be cheerful, then every time you overcome your sad character and are cheerful and positive, you reach a higher spiritual level than a person who is naturally happy.

The Good in Evil

The classic Jewish response to why there is evil in the world is that God wanted to give us the greatest good, but we are by nature embarrassed to receive something for free. This innate embarrassment is referred in Kabbalah as the "bread of shame." We simply do not take pleasure in freebies. It damages our self-respect. We want to work for what we have and get what we deserve. Therefore, God created evil so that we could struggle with it, overcome it, and choose the good. In this way, we earn our goodness, which offers us the greatest satisfaction and pleasure.

When I first heard this teaching, I had a hard time with it. I could not understand why God couldn't have created us without this bread of shame. Certainly, God could have created us without this need. But then I started to think, "Who is it that is feeling this bread of shame?" And I realized that it's the soul, which itself is really an expression of God in this world.

The highest Torah value is justice—when we get what we deserve. We have free will so we can make choices, and based upon our choices, we work hard, put in the effort, overcome obstacles, and earn what we have.

You might ask: "Well then what about God? Can God earn the right to become God? Does God have to deal with the bread of shame? Does God have the opportunity to choose to become God—to earn the right to be God?" The answer is yes—through you and me.

The Kabbalah teaches that although God is already good and whole, God also wants to justifiably achieve goodness and wholeness through struggle, choice, and hard work. We seemingly mere earthlings are this aspect of God that seeks to earn and deserve the ranking of divinity through struggle, choice, and hard work. All our flaws, weaknesses, and problems are absolutely essential to fulfilling our divine destiny. Our divine purpose on Earth is to overcome the bad and boldly choose to become good, whole, and godly (I explain this profound truth in greater depth in my book *The Secret Life of God*.)

There is a cryptic verse in the book of Genesis that states: "And He (God) called him (Jacob) the Lord, God of Israel."[2] The Talmud explains that God actually called Jacob, "God."[3] Jacob is the first model of true self-actualization. This supreme identity, however, awaits us all. The Talmud teaches that in the future all upright virtuous people will be called by the name God.[4]

We can now understand what is good about all our bad. The bad in us and in the world offers us the opportunity to overcome evil and choose good, which is considered to be a much higher form of goodness then mere goodness that simply is and always was. When we see our life in that light we can see and appreciate what is positive about our faults. Our faults create the opportunity to rise to the challenge, choose goodness, and become godly. We can freely choose to be kind, sensitive, and loving because we are challenged with being hateful, greedy, and mean.

This is the theme of life. It's all about choosing the good and through determined hard work earning and deserving the status of godliness. All the players on the field (all our faults, vices, and problems) play an essential part in our greater purpose, which is to achieve godliness through free choice. Remember this truth and it will fill your darkest moments with dazzling hope. God is always on your side because in truth you are expressing a side of God. God is always rooting for you because your true self is rooted in God. Bring this truth into your heart, make it your daily prayer:

I am a part of God with a divine mission to choose the good. All my faults are only opportunities to achieve more, all my bad traits are challenges offering me opportunities to grow and choose to do better. It is all for the good. I am part of the glorious grandeur of God seeking to become manifest in this world.

Summary

Each and every one of us is an individualized expression of the collective soul of his or her nation, which itself is a unique expression of the Universal Soul—God. When we are spiritually healthy we intuit our godly greatness and know that selflessly serving our people, the world, and God is the only true way to self-actualization. We, however, must always remind ourselves that the grandeur we sense inside us is not *our* greatness but God's. How can we know when prideful thoughts are coming from our big ego or from the greatness of our soul as an expression of God? Egomaniacs believe in themselves but only in themselves and simply want to *look* good. Truly humble people, however, believe in themselves because they are a part of God and have a burning desire to do good and *be* good.

The Kabbalah teaches that although God is already good and whole, God also wants to justifiably achieve goodness and wholeness through struggle, choice, and hard work. We seemingly mere earthlings embody this aspect of God. All our flaws, weaknesses, and problems are absolutely essential to fulfilling our divine destiny—to overcome them and boldly choose to become good, whole, and godly. Because we express a side of God we can know for sure that God is always on our side and at our side. When we know and live this truth we enjoy profound serenity and inner peace precisely in the midst of our daily challenges and struggles.

7

Serenity, Here and Now

WHEN THE WORLD TRADE CENTER came down in New York in the terrorist attack of September 11, 2001, people were shaken up the world over. Those two pillars were not just towers; they were symbols of stability. They were pillars of what we call "securities" in American society. The world's financial foundations, as some people understand them, disappeared. And life suddenly felt so fleeting.

One day we woke up and the only thing for sure was that nothing was for sure. Thousands of people went to work one day, and they expected the ordinary—just another day. But it was not. It was possibly the beginning of a whole new period in history.

The world today is experiencing tremendous anxiety. During the Palestinian intifada in Israel where I live, life was fraught with anxiety. You walked out of your door and had no idea what your day was going to bring. I thought about that every day my children would go to school. Some of them took buses. As I said goodbye to them, I did not really know what would be. Was this, "Goodbye, I'll see you tonight" or just, "Goodbye"?

We just did not know. People headed for a family outing, and they did not come back. Every parked car was suspicious. (It is one thing to be suspicious of people, but cars?) Who knew? Any car could hold a bomb. So you walked next to cars, and you wondered why they were parked there. You just realized that you could never know.

When I traveled giving seminars in North America, my family

usually stayed with my in-laws who lived in Beit El, one of the communities in what has been referred to as "the occupied territories." My wife and I always discussed how they should get there. Should they take the bus, which is bullet proof? Then again, terrorism was getting so advanced that buses were prime targets. Maybe they should take a taxi. Then again, there were shootings on the road. Either way, it was a high risk. So we lived with the daily anxiety of not knowing.

Nothing is certain, everything is transient and impermanent, and you never know what could be. I remember when John Lennon was shot. Why was I so shocked? People get shot and die all the time. But John Lennon! The theme song for his memorial special was called, "The Dream Is Over." And it hit me so strongly that you can be famous, larger than life, and you are still going to die.

The Talmud tells a story about two rabbis who make a deal with each other. The one who dies first must come back and tell the other one how it went. So one of them dies and the other one waits for him to visit.

That night, the dead friend comes to him in a dream. The live rabbi is very curious: "How are you doing?" he asks. "What was death like?"

"Death wasn't so bad," the dead rabbi says.

"No?"

"No, the angel of death pulled me out of my body like a hair being pulled out of cream. It was so smooth."

"Wow!" his friend marvels.

"But," the dead rabbi continues, "I do have to tell you something. If they decree upon me to come back to this world, boy, will I put up a fight."

"Why is that?" the second one wonders.

"Because it's not death that worries me, it's the fear of death that worries me."

Death happens once, and most of us will die without even knowing that we were going to die. It is not the moment of death that frightens us most, but the daily fear of death. The fear of death provokes more anxiety and is more difficult to deal with than death itself.

The Great Escape

The truth is that this anxiety is not new at all. Death is old news. So is poverty, disease, and suffering. So then why are there periods when we feel more anxious and worried about them and periods when we don't? We have always been under threat, but we succeed in distracting ourselves from all the anxiety. Much of our culture and modern technology focuses precisely on how to escape pain, fear, and anxiety.

Because my mother was a Holocaust survivor, I grew up very aware of the suffering of the Jewish people and the terrible things that could happen to anybody. I was quite conscious of the transience of life, and it bothered me greatly. In fact, there were nights when I had a hard time sleeping. If it were not for my stereo with the big speakers on each side of my bed blasting rock and roll, I would not have been able to sleep. I spent my life running away from the anxiety of the transience of my life and trying to hardrock myself to sleep.

And that is really what our escapist society is all about—providing painkillers and amusements that serve to put us to sleep. Our escapist society seeks to make us comfortably numb because the more sensitive we are and the more attuned we are, the greater our anxiety about the fragility of life. We spend so much of our life running away from life.

Even today, when I am in the United States and I cannot fall asleep because of jet lag, I turn on the TV to the comedy channels. I love to laugh and I love to help people laugh, but so much of this TV comedy I do not find funny at all. The camera is focused on the people in the audience, who are hysterical, and I am trying to figure out what is wrong with me that I do not think it is funny. I think people go to these comedies determined to laugh. Inside they have decided: "No matter what this guy says, we are going to laugh; if we are going to survive we must laugh."

King Solomon wrote an amazing work called the Book of Ecclesiastes, which is potentially the most depressing book you will ever read, because it takes you through exactly what everybody tries to do in order to cope with their transience and anxiety. It begins: "All is futile!"[1] In Hebrew, the word "futile" is *hevel,* which can also mean vanity, emptiness, or vapor. It reminds me of a cold day when you can see your breath, which looks like something but it is really nothing. This is exactly what King Solomon is struggling with in his book. Everything in life looks so permanent, so solid, but you know it really is not. Plus, everything seems to be going around in circles—the sun rises only to set, and there is nothing new under the sun. Nothing lasts. King Solomon describes the various ways that people have for trying to deal with—or more accurately, to run away from so they don't have to deal with—the excruciating pain of uncertainty, of living a life of constant insecurity.

Can we ever find serenity and inner peace living a life that is so uncertain, so full of anxiety? The general answer that you hear is, "I can cope as long as good times await. If life is not good now, at least it is going to get better soon." With this attitude, serenity and inner peace depend upon the promise of a good future.

So many people live their lives for their vacations. How many times have you heard something similar to this: "Right now, I hate my job and I don't like the people I'm hanging out with, but I know that my vacation in Bermuda is coming in six months. I will get through this terrible time because in six months I'll be happy. Sure, it's only a five-day holiday, but then I can look forward to my summer vacation in the Caribbean."

There are different variations on this attitude. Some people accept that there are no guarantees so they pack in as many pleasures as fast as possible. My wife was at the funeral of her cousin, a young woman who died of cancer. As they were lowering her coffin into the grave, another cousin nodded his head and said,

"That's it, that's what life is. From dust to dust, so you just have to seize the day. Get what you can while you can, live it up now."

This is a common attitude and is as old as civilization. The Roman motto was: "Eat, drink, and be merry, for tomorrow we will die." And since we know that tomorrow we will die, we can sacrifice the future as it is uncertain. All we know is the present, so why not live it up now. Who can say what tomorrow will bring? The comedian Steven Wright puts it this way: "Sure hard work pays off in the future but laziness pays off now. Drugs get you nowhere but at least it's the scenic route."

Many people live their lives for the moment. And there are some who will even give up their dignity and integrity for a fleeting pleasure. But there is another attitude people take in their struggle with the anxiety of the transience of life. They posit, "I'm not going to live for this passing moment, that's silly. I'm going to forfeit the moment for the future. I'm going to give up the fun and pleasures of this transient world for the promise of the great eternal rewards in the next world. I will surrender the now for the later, the moment for an everlasting future."

So which one of these approaches solves the problem? "Seize the day, live for now, and forget about the future?" Or is it, "Better to suffer now and wait for the eternal reward in the world to come?"

To Serve Here and Now

It may surprise you to hear that the Torah approach to life is actually closer to "seize the day" than "wait for eternal reward in afterlife"—though with some serious modifications to what I described above. The Torah teaches us to live for the moment, but to cram into it everlasting meaning.

The "wait for eternal reward in afterlife" approach is closer to the view of Muslim fundamentalists. Muslim terrorist organizations recruit suicide bombers with the promise of a huge reward in heaven—a harem of seventy-two virgins, luxurious cars, and palatial mansions. And because many Muslims live in terrible poverty, feeling terrible despair, they are persuaded by these fantasies.

If you read carefully the Five Books of Moses, you will see there no mention of a world to come or of any reward in the afterlife. Only later, in the books of the prophets, do we find mention to the Messianic Age—when the lion will lie down with the lamb—the arrival of which is not painted in rosy colors.

So Torah tradition does not teach us to live for the future or for the promise of some physical reward in heaven. The sages in *Pirkei Avot*, referred to in English as *Ethics of the Fathers,* advise: "Do not serve the Great One (God) in order to get a prize. You should serve the Great One in order not to get a prize."[2] By this they mean that we should serve God because it is the right thing to do here and now, without any hope or interest in receiving some future reward.

A participant in one of our recent Isralight retreats told me that she desperately wanted to meet her soul mate. "Rabbi, if I start keeping Shabbat, will God give me my soul mate?"

I told her, "There are a lot of people who are incredible Jews and who follow Torah law in every aspect of their lives, and they are still struggling, and some of them are not married though they want to be. You can't decide to celebrate Shabbat for that reason."

I have met other people like her who labor under the misapprehension that embracing religion will erase all their pain. But it does not work that way. Sometimes it works just the opposite. Sometimes, embracing a God-centered life means taking on more challenges.

When I was studying Torah with the actor Kirk Douglas, he was very excited with the learning and his personal growth. Soon he decided that he would light Shabbat candles and that he would not eat pork anymore. These were very big moves for him, but in the middle of it all he had a stroke. Here he was, returning to God, returning to Judaism, and he had a stroke.

God does not promise, certainly not in the immediate future, that because we embrace the Torah our lives will be smooth and easy. But the Torah is not about living for the Messianic Age and the everlasting world to come. The Torah teaches us to seize the day, live in the moment, because all we really have is now. This is what the great sage Hillel taught: "If not now, when?" There is only now. The past is a memory and the future is a dream. They are just mental conceptual abstractions. Only the now is real. Therefore, live for today—make each second of your life count.

The question really is: "How do we truly live for the now? How do we make every moment the most incredible, beautiful, powerful, meaningful moment of our lives?"

The secret to serenity, inner peace, meaning, and ultimate fulfillment is to turn life into a loving service of the Ultimate Self, the Great I—God. We internalize the eternal when we serve God and thereby embody eternal divine values and ideals. A life of love and service means serving to channel through us the loving presence of the Great I, revealing the infinite and eternal within the finite and temporal.

Selling Serenity for Beans

Unfortunately most people are living a life of fear. Fear is about the future. We do something because we are afraid of what might happen, what we might lose or what we could gain. Love is about the present. When we do something out of love, we do it because we feel and want to express love now. If you do a good deed now, it is because you love God now, and you know that this is an opportunity to experience and make manifest divine love. It has nothing to do with the future. It offers you the ever-present joy of living a fulfilled life here and now, loving God and your fellow human beings.

The Torah teaches us to seize the day and live in the moment. Don't waste time on lusts that don't last. The worst thing that could ever happen to your lustful desires is to fulfill them because as soon as you do they will be gone. Anticipating your desires is more pleasurable than actually fulfilling them, because in a flash they are gone. Desires expire but love lasts. We live it up in the moment when we love and serve in the moment.

This attitude is what marked the difference between Jacob and his brother Esau. The Torah tells us that one day when Esau came home from being out in the field hunting, he saw his brother Jacob cooking a red bean stew, and said to him (I paraphrase here):

"What's that red stuff, brother? Pour it down my throat—I'm so tired, I'm doing to die."

And Jacob replied, "I'll give it to you, but in exchange I want your birthright." And indeed, the Torah relates, Esau sold his birthright to Jacob for beans.[3]

The Midrash fills in the dialogue. Esau said to Jacob, "I don't understand! Why do you want the birthright? Why is it so important to be the first born?"

"Because the first born is going to have the opportunity to serve God in the Holy Temple," Jacob answered.

"What's the big deal about serving that?"

"I'll tell you a little bit about what it means, Esau. If you enter the Holy Temple to serve God but your hair is disheveled, you would be liable to the death penalty."

Esau was a hairy fellow so he said in dismay, "Oh, yeah?"

Jacob continued, "And if you enter the Temple drunk, you could also be liable to the death penalty."

Jacob then proceeded to tell Esau all the stringent laws that the Temple priest would have to abide by during the service.

Esau realized that his birthright was going to kill him, because everything he liked would be forbidden. He thought, "If serving God takes all the fun out of life—who needs it?" So he sold his birthright for beans.

From this Midrash, we may find it easier to understand Esau's attitude than Jacob's. Why would we want a life that has so many restrictions and laws that are punishable by death?

Jacob knew something about the Torah that Esau did not. The Torah is called the *Etz Chaim,* the "Tree of Life." It is almost impossible to be subjected to the death penalty in Torah law because the rulings of the court and the details and the necessities of what it takes to pass such a judgment are so specific that the chances of a death sentence ever being passed is practically nil.

In a true Torah court it is nearly impossible to ever get the death penalty and it rarely ever happened. So if this is true—and capital punishment is essentially theoretical—then why does the Torah mention the death penalty so much?

I once heard an incredible answer to this question from one of my teachers. He explained that the Torah talks about the death penalty to tell us how much life is in it if we live it. The Torah wants to communicate to us in the most dramatic way that if some violation of Shabbat could be theoretically punishable by death, then imagine how much life there is in celebrating Shabbat.

Jacob understood this. Esau, however, felt that if he followed the commandments of the Torah he would be giving up the good life. Esau believed in "eat, drink, and be merry, for tomorrow we may die," while Jacob believed in "eat, drink, and be merry, but invite God to join you and turn it into loving service."

Jacob understood that the good life is when you have God in your life. Jacob and Esau both agreed there is no time like the present and you have to seize the moment, enjoy life now and be happy, but they disagreed on how to achieve that. Esau's motto was "Lust while it lasts—so serve yourself here and now." But Jacob's motto was "Only love can ever last. So lovingly serve God here and now."

Embracing the Transient

To infuse each moment with the greatest amount of life force, we must live each moment in service of the Source of life—the Great I. To make each moment ultimate we need to use each moment of our life to love and serve the Ultimate Self and channel God's love, kindness, and goodness to the rest of the world. When we immerse ourselves in each moment to meet God, and we embrace each moment as an opportunity to lovingly serve God and each other, we overcome the anxiety of transience because each moment is then filled with eternal meaning.

This is the lesson of Sukkot (the Festival of Booths), which is one of the most beautiful holidays of the Jewish calendar and which is called "the time of our joy." In celebrating this holiday we are commanded to take up temporary residence in a sukkah, a flimsy hut topped with a sparse amount of perishable plant material so that you can see the stars at night.

Sukkot includes a few other rituals that help us seize the day and be with God. Each day of the holiday we wave the four species—palm branch (called *lulav* in Hebrew), myrtle branches (*hadasim*), willow branches (*aravot*) and a citron (*etrog*). These are held together, close to the heart, and then waved or shaken while verses of praise and thanks to God are chanted.

Right after Yom Kippur—the Day of Atonement—the shopping for Sukkot starts. It is an intense time, especially in Jerusalem. All through the markets, vintage-looking Jews with little gem glasses examine each *etrog* for every little blemish. You see, we want to do this in the most beautiful way. People may even spend hundreds of dollars on these four species, though in a week's time when the holiday ends they will be worth nothing.

During the week of Sukkot we watch the four species that we spent so much money on wilt away. It is a wonder why, in a world with such advanced technology, we cannot create a nice looking plastic *etrog* that we could use every year. Nowadays, we can buy artificial flowers that even smell real. These things last. But on Sukkot we immerse ourselves in a temporary dwelling, we embrace perishable species, and we turn around and wave them toward the four corners of the Earth. It really seems silly; turning in a circle we just end up in the same place that we started.

Also seemingly strange is that during this "time of our joy" we read the Book of Ecclesiastes—definitely sober stuff. The sages tell us that King Solomon was inspired to write this book when he realized in a prophetic way that the Temple that he built would be destroyed. Lamenting over that painful truth he wrote: "All is futile . . . of what worth is the work of man under the sun."[4] It sure seems odd to read this apparently depressing book on the holiday of our happiness. However, King Solomon's brutal confrontation with the transience of life actually reveals the key to true serenity and inner peace. He concludes, "In the end, obey the word of God and do His command because this is everything."[5]

After describing his efforts to find permanence in life, King Solomon realizes the secret to serenity—live in the present, serve God now, and connect to the Great I by lovingly living his will.

On Sukkot we celebrate transience. We embrace transience when we embrace our perishable four species, and we immerse ourselves in transience when we leave our permanent home and dwell in a temporary hut covered by perishable plant material. Sukkot teaches us that serenity and inner peace are not based on what you have nor what you can hold onto but who you are by virtue of your relationship to God. When we love and serve the Great I here and now, make his will our will, we infuse this finite space with infinity and this fleeting moment with eternity.

If you understand this truth then you will never be in a rush to get to some other place and get to some future time. Because you will realize that the joy of life is to love and serve God and there is no better time than now and no better place then here. If not now, when?

Therefore, the key to serenity is to embrace the present, as impermanent as it is. The present is, so to speak, a presentation and manifestation of the Great I in this moment. Our joy is to merge with this moment, fully live it by doing good for and spreading love to each other, lovingly serving God in his desire to become evermore present in our lives and in this world through us.

Summary

How can we overcome the anxiety of our transient lives to find serenity and happiness when the fear of death, uncertainty, and insecurity haunt us daily? Many people simply live it up now and forget about the daunting future. Others, however, believe it is better to sacrifice the worldly pleasures of the now and secure eternal reward in the afterlife by living a prudent ascetic life. The Torah, however, teaches us to live for the moment but cram into it eternal love and everlasting meaning. In other words, serve God here and now. Make his will our will and bring his love, kindness, and goodness to all. Do not, however, do good or refrain from doing wrong because of the fear of what may be lost or gained in the future. The key to serenity is doing good now because we love God and each other now and want to express and experience that love now. We will stop feeling rushed to get to some other place or get to some future time as soon as we realize that there is no better time than now and no better place than here to love and serve God and each other. Serving here and now, however, is not only the key to serenity but also the secret to living a full life where every day is momentous and happiness is our choice.

8

Choosing Happiness, Making Life Momentous

A FEW YEARS AGO I was counseling a couple on the brink of divorce. In a private session with the husband, he related to me that the key problem was his wife's inability to forgive. To illustrate his point, he related to me an event, which as it turned out, happened twenty years ago.

I told him, "She might not be able to forgive, but you can't forget."

Then, in a private session with the wife, she related to me that the key problem was her husband's inability to apologize. To illustrate her point, she related to me the same event as her husband had from twenty years ago.

One of my students, age twenty-eight, told me that his father insulted him when he was twelve and to this day he continues to feel hurt. I explained to him that, although his father hurt him when he was twelve, he has allowed his father to continue to hurt him for another sixteen years by holding on to the pain and constantly remembering it. I suggested that either he confront his father and try to make peace or simply let it go, forget it, and move on.

Not only do we often live in the past and obsess over what no longer is, but we also waste our time by worrying over the future. Imagine that you finally take that vacation to Bermuda you always dreamed about. You are lying on a gorgeous beach next to the clear blue sea but your mind is a cesspool of memories and worries. Although your body is in Bermuda, your thoughts are still back at the office. In your mind you are consumed by the argument you had last week with your boss, hearing every mean sentence he said over and over again. And then you are ridden by anxiety as you envision the confrontation and anticipate every insult he will surely hurtle at you when you return. At the end of your vacation to Bermuda, all you can say is that you were there, but you were not present.

Even the simple pleasures of our daily life are sacrificed to our obsessions and inability to stay focused in the present. How many times do we eat a delicious meal without enjoying even one bite because we are lost in our thoughts about what will be tomorrow? We can be so addicted to thinking about the future that when the future is finally present, we will be absent because we will already be obsessing about what comes next.

How can we stop living in our fantasies of the future or in our memories of the past and start living in the now? The past and the future do not exist. They are merely mental abstractions of our minds. Only the now is real. Only the now is alive. Our life is only happening right now. We can only live our lives in the present. And when we live fully in the now we infuse life into our living. To truly be alive we need to be fully present in the now.

Making Each Day Count

The Torah tells us that the matriarch Sarah lived for 127 years. But the wording is very strange. It literally reads, "And the life of Sarah was 127 years; these were the years of the life of Sarah."[1] Why this odd repetition?

The sages explain that the years of Sarah's life equaled the years that she actually *lived*. In other words, a person may die at age 127 and even though her life *lasted* 127 years, she did not *live* 127 years. She may have only lived ten years of her life and wasted the rest. Some people live a long life but not a full life. Sarah lived a long and full life. The number of years she lived equaled the number of years of her life.

The Torah teaches that already at birth our days are numbered. It is up to us to make each day count. How can we do that? How can we choose life and live in the now? The secret to living a full life is *kavana*—"intention/concentration/focus." *Kavana* requires us to be focused human beings, concentrating on the here and now. Then life becomes alive.

Most of us, however, live fractured lives. We might be here, but our minds are over there; our bodies are in the present, but our minds are in the past or the future. We need to give our undivided attention to the present because this is when life is happening— right here and right now. Here and now is the only place and time we can meet each other and meet God.

Some people mistakenly think that they will meet God in the future, in the afterlife, in heaven. However, the truth is that if they can't meet God here and now, then they will not be able to meet God there and then.

The Future and the Past

If life only happens in the present, then what is meaning of the past and the future? The Torah talks a lot about the importance of remembering the past and planning for the future. For one, we are commanded to remember the miraculous escape of the Jewish people from their slavery in Egypt. All the Jewish holidays commemorate past events in history. The Torah also encourages us to always remember the wrongdoings of our past. Furthermore, the Baal Shem Tov, the eighteenth-century founder of the Hassidic movement, teaches that forgetfulness leads to exile while remembrance is the secret of redemption.

As for the future, we are obligated to anticipate daily the arrival of the Messiah and the Final Redemption. The Talmud also teaches that a wise person is someone who has foresight.[2] And the writings of the prophets are filled with predictions for the future.

Of course, our abilities to remember the past and predict the future enrich our lives, but they can also destroy our lives. God intended us to use these powers to live fully in the moment, not to abuse these powers and destroy the moment. If your expectations for the future can help you fully live in the moment and take advantage of the moment, then you are using your tools wisely. But if you are talking to someone and your mind is wandering to a conversation that you are going to have with someone else tomorrow, your expectations for the future are causing you to waste time now—this is not helpful; this is destructive.

I cannot remember how many conversations I have had in my head with people before I met them. And when I finally had the actual discussion with them, they did not remotely say what I expected them to say. Of course, at that point, I could not say what I planned to say. It was a totally ridiculous use of my time and brainpower.

Unique to human beings is our memory of the past and anticipation of the future. Animals live completely in the moment. They do not get anxious, they do not obsess, they live completely in the moment and they seem happy. Rabbi Isaac Blauzer, one of the great leaders of the Mussar Movement (the great ethical movement of the nineteenth century) encouraged his students to learn from animals how to live in the moment. Animals have no worries or anxieties, they simply focus on the here and now. He further pointed out that although it is humiliating for a human being to learn from an animal, it is even more humiliating not to learn from them.

Animals live in the moment—exactly what we are here to do. We are supposed to use our ability to speculate about the future and to remember the past, but only for one purpose—to help us take full advantage of the present and fully live the unique opportunity of service that the present moment offers. Otherwise, we are wasting our lives by living in our abstractions. We are here but our mind is there; we are now but our mind is tomorrow or yesterday. The Torah teaches, "And you shall know today and bring it into your heart, because the Lord He is God in heaven above, and upon the Earth beneath: there is none else."[3] In other words, when you realize that God is omnipresent—completely here and now—you will intimately know and embrace each day. The great nineteenth-century Hasidic master, Rabbi Nachman of Breslov, in lesson 272 of his *Liqute Maharan,* taught that a fundamental axiom in serving God is to only have the present day in mind.

Yes we have a memory, and we have a dream, but both are meant to help us live the true meaning of the present moment as a link in the chain of time. We must always realize that we live only one moment at a time—this is it, this moment. When we use our memories and our dreams to zero in on the potential service of the moment and immerse ourselves in the moment, our lives will have momentum. But if we are thinking about the past and the future that have nothing to do with the task at hand, then our memory and planning are destructive.

Many people share their problems with me, but sometimes I am not sure that I am helping them. When people talk about what has already happened and what they think is going to happen, I wonder if I am really helping them to live in the moment. Is this conversation going to help them? At these times I feel power-less because we are really just hanging on to memories that are not productive right now and to anticipations of what could be. A person should never say, "I shouldn't have," "I could have," "if only I would have," or "what will happen if." You have to do what you have to do now. Live the service of today. Use the past and the future only to the extent that they help you now: seize the day and the unique service it offers.

Take children, for example. They are happy because they really live in the moment. They absorb themselves completely in what they are doing. Adults are often distracted, while children give their undivided attention to whatever they are playing with at the moment—however short that moment may be.

The other day my year-and-a-half-old son, Shmaya, had to get a flu shot. When we arrived at the clinic, the nurse told me to hold him.

"Where are you going to do?" I asked her.

"I'm going to give him the shot in his thigh because that's the most fleshy part of babies," she informed me.

So, as instructed, I held him, but silly me, I held his legs because she was going to inject the needle in his thigh. At this point, he was drinking his bottle and very happy because he did not know what was about to happen. All he saw was this nice lady nurse. All of a sudden, "OWWWW!"

She had stuck the needle into his thigh, and she started to yell at me: "Hold his hands, hold his hands!" I hadn't anticipated it—of course, the first thing he tried to do was pull the needle out. It was an absolutely horrible experience. But I learned a lesson from it.

One second he is screaming, then the needle is out, the pain is gone, I give him the bottle, and he stops. Just like that. At the poor nurse, however, he just growls. Seeing his attitude, she blows up a rubber glove, ties a knot and draws on it two eyes and a mouth. It looks like a little chicken. She gives it to him, and now he is mesmerized. It has all been forgotten. One moment he is crying, the next moment he is laughing and playing.

Learning to Be Fully Present

Obviously, we evolve. One of the signs of maturity, adulthood, and higher consciousness is the ability to draw from the lessons of the past and to anticipate, predict, and plan the future. It is a good, advanced skill, if it helps us *now*. If it does not, forget about it. Let go of it.

Sure, it is hard, but it is certainly possible. One of the ways that you can forget about it is to immerse yourself in what you are doing. Rabbi Nachman of Breslov taught: "The whole wide world is a very narrow bridge, but the main thing to recall is to have no fear at all."

A story is told about the Hassidic master Rabbi Chaim Krasney who collected all his students together when he heard that a fellow in the town was going to walk across the river on a tightrope. The students were appalled—why would their teacher want them to spend precious time away from Torah study to watch some guy do a circus trick. But they did as they were told and watched Rabbi Chaim studying the man's every step with deep concentration.

Afterward, one of the students says, "Rabbi Chaim, why was that so important?"

Rabbi Chaim answered, "Because we need to learn how to live our lives by watching this fellow's concentration at every step. If he were to start thinking about how much money he was going to get for this or worrying about whether they were going to pay him or what people were thinking of him or what's going to happen tomorrow when he performs again, then he would fall. But he didn't fall because he was completely engrossed in each step. That is how we should live our lives—focused on each step."

This attitude is reflected in the Kabbalah's concept of *tzimtzum* ("contraction" or "concentrated withdrawal"). The Kabbalah teaches that before creation there was just the endless light of God; in other words, the endless manifestation and presence of the Great I. God, however, contracted his endless light and withdrew it, moved himself away from the center while making a space for the creation of vessels. (The vessels refer to time, space, matter, and you and me.) God then projected a thin ray of his endless light into the vessels. This process of making a space and infusing every moment, every place, and everyone with the presence of the Great I is the mystery and miracle of the *tzimtzum*. We, too, must perform this divine act in the service of God. First, we have to move everything out of the way, get rid of the racket and then we must bracket this moment and this place.

I could be speaking with my daughter but not be able to hear her because although she is right in front of me, in my mind I am thinking about someone else, a person who hurt me yesterday or a person who will come see me tomorrow. To be there for my daughter I have to push these thoughts away and make a space in my life for my daughter. This is the first part of *tzimtzum*.

Now that I have pushed everything else away and created a space for her in the center, I have to concentrate my entire being into the here and now and be fully present for my daughter and invest my entire self into this moment. That is the power of *tzimtzum*—the power of concentration and the art of being fully present.

My fondest memories of my childhood are the times when my mother would read to me from *Winnie the Pooh*. Since my mother was from Poland, she pronounced it as "Vinnie the Pew." When I later spoke to my school friends about "Vinnie the Pew," they thought he was some mafia leader. But that did not spoil it for me because when my mother would read to me those were incredible magical moments. Although my parents bought me all kinds of toy trains and squirt guns, I realized that there is no greater gift than the gift of presence. My mother put everything else out of her mind, put me in the center of her attention, and infused those moments with her entire presence. She was completely there for me, and I felt loved. The art of *tzimtzum* is the secret to love and happiness.

Where You Are Is Where God Is

"In all your ways, know Him (God)," King Solomon teaches in the Book of Proverbs.[4] Our sages tell us that this statement really captures the essence of a life. The Hebrew words *b'chol drecheha daiehu* ("in all your ways, know Him") can also be translated as "with every step of your journey, you must know Him." In other words, you must focus your attention on every step you take in your life to know God. And the only place you can make I-contact—meet and know the Great I—is right here, right now—wherever you are and in whatever you are doing. Wherever you are in your journey that is where God is because God is with you every step of the way.

I once saw a bumper sticker over a friend's kitchen sink that read, "I'D RATHER BE LEARNING TORAH." This kind of thinking destroys life. The Torah teaches us that we can and must serve God and connect with the Great I in whatever we are doing.

If you have to do dishes now, and this is your responsibility, then this is your service and through it you can know God. Focus on the miraculous coordination of your hands, the beautiful fragrance of the soap, marvel over the funky colors in the bubbles, be thankful that you have dishes to eat on. If you are eating, God is there at your meal. Savor each bite, chew your food, completely enjoy the taste, contemplate the wonders of your entire digestive system, fill yourself with gratitude that you have food to eat. Don't shove the food down your throat so that you can just finish your meal and get on with reading a holy book. Make your meal a service. The sages teach that eating is a holy service and the table is like the altar in the Temple. God is right here at your table and at your meal right now. If you are praying, you should be completely immersed in your prayers. And when you are learning Torah, you should be giving yourself over completely to that learning, because God is with you right here, right now.

Only here and only now can we serve and meet the Great I. This is paramount to being alive.

Making Each Moment Momentous

The son of a friend of mine died at a young age from a terminal disease. Knowing that he would die before he reached thirty, he told his mother, "Mom, I might not live a long life, but I will live a full life." This is the point: It is not about a long life, it is about a full life. You cannot have a full life unless you are fully immersed in what you are doing right now and turning it into an opportunity to lovingly serve and know God.

The problem is that the modern world often pulls at us from all sides. There are people who cannot eat without reading the newspaper and talking on the phone at the same time. Wait a second: If you are eating, then eat! Enjoy every morsel; now it is time to eat. There is a time to talk and a time to plan. What are you doing now?

Abraham is one of the best examples of a person who was totally immersed in what he was doing. The Book of Genesis describes him sitting in his tent when he sees three strangers approaching. He immediately runs to greet them and invite them to dinner.

The Torah—a book that does not waste words—is very specific in telling us everything he does in this episode, where it could have summed it up in one sentence. Instead, the Torah gives us a play-by-play description.

The Torah wants us to understand that Abraham was fully immersed in every move he made. The point was not that he fed his guests but that he attended to their needs at every moment. Sure, Abraham had lots of important things he could have been doing, but once he had a guest in front of him, he was completely with his guest, right here, right now. And this is why the Torah introduces the story with "And God appeared to him"; Abraham served God in the here and now by serving his guests.

There is a teaching in Eastern tradition that proclaims, "Be here and now." The Torah, however, would say, "Serve God here and now." This is the fullest experience of life.

To serve God is to imbue each moment with the presence of the Great I. God wants to be present in the here and now, and our job is to serve God in that desire. In other words, we should ask ourselves: "How can I serve God right now?" If right now I imbue this moment with God's wisdom, I am serving the Great I. If right now I am with my son, I should see this moment as an opportunity to show him love and thus serve God, who is the source of all love. It's not my love. I didn't invent love. I didn't create love and I didn't give it its power and meaning. Love did not start with me and love will not end with me. I am not the master of love, but I am the servant of love. And when I love my son I serve the Great I to become present in the here and now.

My service to God—who wants to be present in this world right now—is to bring his love into this moment—or his compassion and justice if that is what he wants of me in this moment. This is the secret to living a full life; a life of holiness. We should not be living in the past or for the future. The goal of life is to be fully present in this moment, serving God—here and now—in spreading and sharing his love and goodness. There is no greater fulfillment or joy in life than this. God wants to be present in this world through you and me. To live is to lovingly serve. This is our ultimate accomplishment and joy.

If you are on the beach playing Frisbee and you ask yourself, "Am I having fun?" then you are definitely not having fun because it means that you are not fully absorbed in the moment. If you are sitting by the sea, listening to the enchanting sound of the waves, and you ask yourself, "Am I experiencing serenity and inner peace now?" then you are definitely not because you are not fully present. You could not be fully there if you could ask the question.

The highest expression of pleasure is the unconsciousness of self. The greatest source of pain is self-consciousness. If I am self-conscious, then I am not completely absorbed in the moment. When you are reading a good book, are you aware that you are reading a good book? No, you are just absorbed in reading a good book. You don't stop to notice and take your temperature, so to speak.

A story is told in Hassidic literature about a young yeshiva student who used to pray with so much enthusiasm that he would stomp his foot without realizing it. Normally, this would pose no problem. But the boy had a lame foot. One day, his rabbi's wife said to her husband, "Please tell the youngster not to stomp his lame foot because he could really aggravate his malady."

The rabbi said to her, "If I thought he knew which foot he was stomping, I would tell him. But he's in such a state of ecstasy, he's so completely absorbed in his prayers, he doesn't even know he's stomping on his bad foot."

Where there is no self-consciousness, when we are completely absorbed in the moment in our service to God, we become one with the Great I. Making I-contact is sheer ecstasy.

Happiness Is a Choice

Someone asked me if we could always be happy. The answer is, yes, we can always be happy, even when we are crying. If now is the time to be crying, then you should be happy that you know how to cry. It would be really sad if you are at a funeral and while the moment calls for heartfelt tears you instead are laughing.

A woman once came to my office and told me that she could not cry. From the look on her face, you could see that she was very tough. I soon discovered the reason why. When her father died she did not go to the funeral. She went to work as usual because she did not want to deal with his death. She went into complete denial. Her choice not to deal with what was happening right then made her so hard that she could not cry ever. In truth it would have made her so happy had she embraced her sadness and cried because that is what the moment called for.

True happiness does not mean you are upbeat all the time. From the Book of Ecclesiastes we learn that there is a time for war, there is a time for love, there is a time for dancing, there is a time for mourning, and so forth. We are happy when we know which time it is because only then are we serving the Great I according to the unique call of the moment.

Let's say that in this moment we are with a friend who just lost a loved one. Certainly we are serving God—spreading and sharing his compassion and empathy—when we comfort the mourner. But if in the next moment things are going great, then we serve God by making present his joyfulness.

Most of us, however, do not know what the moment calls for. We are not tuned in to the ever-present voice of God trying to get our attention. Because we are thinking so much about the past and the future those times are more real than the present. When we are not present in the now we miss God's presence. And the pain that we may have experienced thirty years ago continues to hurt, despite the fact that no one is actively hurting us anymore. True, it is hard to forget pain, but there is a way. Choose to find in every moment the divine attribute that you can serve to make manifest in light of the present situation. Happiness is sure to result when we serve to reveal God's presence here and now.

The Talmud teaches that only a service-driven life provides happiness. And there is no situation or challenge that does not offer us the opportunity to embody godly attributes and channel Divine Presence. When we live a life of service we are revealing God's presence in the world in the appropriate way the moment calls for.

In Ethics of the Fathers (*Pirkei Avot*), the sages advise that one hour of penitence and good deeds in this world is equal to the entirety of the next world.[5] Can you imagine that?

Torah places more emphasis on living for this world than for the next, in the afterlife. In fact, our focus should be to bring the peacefulness of the next world *into* this world; to completely immerse ourselves in what we are doing right now and not be in a rush. In other words, living a life full of concentration—of undivided attention, where we are not separated from the moment and not divided inside ourselves or from each other or from God.

People live their lives on fast forward, when they should really be living on deep inward, serving God by revealing his goodness, spreading his love, and embodying the divine qualities of wisdom, understanding, compassion, love, justice, truth, mastery, magnificence, and peace in the world. (We will discuss this in greater detail in the next chapter.) When we serve God here and now, we make these qualities present in every moment. That's what we came to this world to do and that's the only reason we are here.

There is nothing to look forward to in the future that this moment cannot offer you. You can serve the Great I now and in any situation. When you are breaking up with your boyfriend or girlfriend, you can serve God by expressing understanding, compassion, and truth. When you are losing your job, you can serve God by showing love and accepting justice. When you are giving birth, you can serve God by knowing that you are bringing life into the world. If you are single or if you are married, you can serve God right now. Do you think that you can serve God better when you're married than when you are single? If right now you are single, this is how you are supposed to serve God. And if and when you get married, then that's how you will serve God. Happiness is a choice available to us all because in whatever situation we find ourselves, we can choose to be of service and channel the presence of God into the here and now. Every day of our life can be purposeful and meaningful, passionately doing good and spreading love.

I once met a woman who told me that she would rather be dead than single the rest of her life. I asked her whether there was anything meaningful and fulfilling that she could do in her life as a single person. She said no.

I explained to her that her desperation to get married may be interfering with her success in meeting a man. To meet someone you have to be present. You can't be present if, while you are conversing with your date, you are thinking about the next date and wondering if this man is likely to put a ring on your finger.

I asked this woman how she knew that she would be happily married. I have met quite a lot of miserable married couples who dream about the good times when they were single. She was certain that would not happen to her.

I am not sure. If you'd rather be dead than single then you are not basing the meaning of your life on serving God. And you missed the point of life, which is to lovingly serve God here and now and make I-contact. This is the key to living a happy, purposeful, meaningful, committed, and serene life in whatever situation you are in.

Summary

To live a full life we not only need to "be here and now," but also to "serve here and now." We often live our lives on fast forward, when we should really be living our lives on deep inward. We must master the art of *tzimtzum*—push away the racket and concentrate our entire being on serving, here and now, God and each other. King Solomon teaches in the Book of Proverbs, "In all your ways, know Him (God)." In other words, seek to serve God and connect with the Great I wherever you are in your journey and in whatever you are doing because God is with you in every step of the way.

God, the Great Self, wants to be present in this world here and now through you and me. Our ultimate accomplishment and joy is to serve that purpose; to imbue each moment with Divine Presence—godly wisdom, love, truth, and so on. When we are completely absorbed in the moment of our service to God, bringing blessing to all, we become one with God, make I-contact, and experience sheer ecstasy.

When we embrace this truth we realize that happiness is a choice. In whatever situation we find ourselves, we can always choose to lovingly serve in channeling the presence of God into the here and now and make our lives momentous.

Indeed the service-driven life is the path to personal fulfillment. Living it, however, takes more than just an attitude. We need a daily spiritual fitness plan to get our souls in shape and get to work.

9

Getting Our Souls in Shape

THERE WAS ONCE a new shopping mall that opened up in Canada, but the traffic into the building was less than hoped for. The owners decided to offer free food in order to attract more people. And indeed the free food drew a great crowd, and they quickly doubled the number of visitors to the new mall. But that didn't help sales. In fact, they found that sales were even lower than what they were when they had fewer people. Then they realized that people buy less on a full stomach. So if you want to save money be sure to eat before you go shopping. Because both shopping and eating are about consumption. When people feel empty, they try to fill that emptiness with food or other things. But that seldom, if ever, satisfies the deeper source of their gnawing need. The soul does not crave *things,* and things will not satiate it. The soul only craves *no-things*.

I once saw a great bumper sticker that read: "The best things in life are not things." We hope to somehow fill our souls with things, but our souls are not nurtured by things. Love is not a thing. It's very real, but it's not a thing. Meaning is not a thing, but it's very real. When people feel that meaning in their lives is gone, they may actually consider committing suicide. Even if they have everything and lack nothing, they are still missing the no-things in life. When everything isn't enough, then it is time to seek the greater no-things.

Animals are easily made happy—food and shelter generally does it—and, as long as no one is hurting them, they're satisfied.

But because we are souls, because we are godly beings, we crave godliness in our lives and all the no-things divinity engenders.

I once met a fellow who was in twelve-step recovery, and he told me that in his program he was taught a saying: "There's a God-sized hole in everyone, and only God can fill that hole."

This is the meaning of the Kabbalistic story known as the "breaking of the vessels." The Kabbalah teaches that, when creating life, God first formed finite vessels into which he poured the endless light of his presence, but the vessels could not handle so much divinity, and they broke. The obvious question is: "Why then did God give his endless light to the vessels when surely he knew that they did not have the capacity to receive and hold it?" The answer is that God wanted to give us a taste of him, so that we would crave his presence in our lives and join together—mending the vessels—to once again receive his endless light and this time be able to hold onto it.

Looking for Fulfillment

We are all looking for fulfillment, but what is that exactly? What does being "fulfilled" mean? Isn't it a strange thing to say? I want to be *full-filled*. It clearly states that I want to be "filled" with the "full." What's the full? Who's the full?

In the Jewish tradition, one of the words that allude to the divine is *kol*—the "all." It means that God's presence fills the whole world and encompasses the whole world. God is the fullness of life—the whole that is greater than the sum of its parts.

The Book of Genesis states that Abraham was blessed *b'kol,* "in all"; Isaac was blessed *m'kol,* "from all"; and Jacob was blessed with *kol,* "all":

And Abraham was old and far advanced in age, and God had blessed Abraham in all . . . Isaac trembled violently, and said, ". . . I have eaten from all before you came" . . . Jacob said, ". . . Please take the gift that I brought to you, because God has dealt graciously with me, and because I have all."[1]

Jacob was very worried about meeting his brother, Esau, who had repeatedly threatened to kill him. But Esau had a change of heart and when they finally met after many years, they greeted each other warmly. Jacob wanted to give his brother a gift, but Esau responded, "I have plenty, my brother; let that which you have be yours. I don't need your gift." But Jacob insisted: "Please take the gift that I brought to you because God has dealt graciously with me, and because I have it all."[2]

How can anybody have it all? How could Jacob say that he has everything? Indeed, looking at his life, we might tend to doubt it. He had one problem after another. First he had to flee from his home because his brother wanted to kill him, and he was a fugitive for many years. Then, living with his father-in-law, Laban, he was repeatedly lied to and cheated—first over the young woman he wanted to marry, then over the sheep he tended. But yet he insisted he had it "all."

According to the Kabbalah, the Hebrew word *kol* is a code for God's presence in our life—the "all." When you feel you have all, you feel satisfied, *full.* That's a godly experience.

That is why we want to be full-filled. And what is fulfillment? It's not plenty of money or things. I have met lots of hungry millionaires. They have lots of money, beautiful clothing, and palatial homes but they don't feel full-filled. Of course, if all that is used to enhance the spiritual quality of one's life, then it could be a vehicle for fulfillment. But if it doesn't, then it can actually be a curse. There's no wealth in that money. Like the saying goes: "Many poor souls live in million-dollar mansions." I remember meeting a woman who was a multimillionaire, and she said to me, "My money is destroying my marriage; it's destroying my children."

But if a person takes his money and all the things he owns and uses them to bring into the world God's presence (and all the divine no-things it engenders), then such a person is truly wealthy.

His money and property have true value. He has it all, he has the "all."

The Kabbalah offers us a real way to draw true abundance into our lives and feel fulfilled—that is, filled with the fullness of God's presence. It teaches us that there are ten *sefirot* (powers or channels of Divine Presence that fill the world). The ten *sefirot* are ten no-things. Through these ten no-things the endless light of God's presence that fills all becomes manifest in our daily lives.

Love is a no-thing. God is love. However, although God is love, love is not God because God is also justice, but justice is not God because God is also truth. But truth is not God because God is also kindness, and beauty, and wisdom, and on and on, and beyond. All these spiritual qualities are really manifestations of the divine.

We all yearn—whether we are aware of it or not, whether we call ourselves religious or atheistic or even anti-religious—to have the presence of God in our lives. Because we all want meaning, we all want purpose, we all want love. These are not things. These are all the divine no-things of life.

How do we access them? By channeling God's presence into the world through what we think, say, and do. This is how we serve and connect with the Great I. And this is the simple secret to profound joy and ultimate fulfillment.

Below is a list that I've developed based on the Kabbalah, which I call the "fulfillment list." It outlines the ten *sefirot*—the divine no-things. These ten no-things are the essential ingredients to living a life of fulfillment. Please note that this list only hints and alludes to the meaning of these divine powers and qualities because they can't quite be captured in words and certainly not in lists. Following the list, we will discuss each of the *sefirot*, explaining how we can channel God's presence via each one.

Keter (crown): Willful, resourceful, unlimited willpower.
Chochma (wisdom): Mindful, purposeful, goal minded, foresight, visionary.

Bina (insight): Insightful, meaningful, strategy minded, practical, analytical, calculating, detail oriented.

Daat (knowledge): Faithful, confident, committed, decisive, strong-willed, intellectually balanced.

Chesed (kindness): Helpful, bountiful, passionate, giving, benevolent, selfless, forthcoming.

Gevurah (discipline):Careful, dutiful, cautious, reserved, law-abiding, controlled, restrained.

Tiferet (inner beauty): Truthful, beautiful, honest, loving, compassionate, emotionally balanced.

Netzach (victory): Powerful, forceful, assertive, persistent, achiever, relentless, bold, tenacious, determined, resolute.

Hod (acknowledgment): Grateful, submissive, accepting, compliant, acquiescent, adaptable, agreeable, yielding.

Yesod (foundation): Peaceful, useful, zestful, joyful, graceful, masterful, successful, realistic, responsible, flexible, grounded, cooperative, coordinated, integrated, down to earth, productive.

Malchut (kingdom): Receptive, humble.

Keter

Keter, which means "crown," is the fountainhead of everything. If you are not connected to keter, then you can't even begin. You know you are connected when you are filled with willpower and desire to act. You are willful. Keter—willpower—is the driving force of your life. Without it nothing in your life can happen. In fact, will is life itself. It takes will to get up in the morning; it takes will to go to work. Will is bombarding you all the time. You actually have no choice when it comes to will.

What you want is your choice, but *that* you want, is not your choice. You always want something or nothing, or someone or maybe no one. Will is constantly pouring into you every single second. If you lost your will completely, you would die. As Rabbi Kook teaches:

The will is the source of life. A person's will is really the foundation for his personal evolution and presence of being. However, will needs development and actualization, more than all the other powers put together.[3]

Viktor Frankl points out the same thing in *Man's Search for Meaning*. He explains, for instance, that if a man lived solely for his wife, his whole life dedicated to her, he would die if she died. He would simply lose his will to live if she died because he could not imagine living without her. The only thing that would save him would be finding another purpose to live for.

The more you want to live, the more alive you actually become and the longer you will live. Medical research shows that patients with fatal illnesses often die after New Year's Day because they have put in their minds that they want to live until the end of the year. It's amazing—the will to live can determine the length of life itself. And, of course, it is a critical factor in healing. Healing is not just in the hands of the doctor or medication—it primarily rests within the willpower of the person, and the worst happens when the person stops wanting to live.

The quality of your life, the vitality of your life is determined by the quality and vitality of your will. Willpower needs to be generated, nurtured, and sustained. Your goals in life have to be worth wanting to draw down a powerful and abundant influx of will.

If you're living for money, sex, or fame that is just not enough to cause the divine life force to pour into you. It is just not enough to draw down the will you need to rise to the real challenges of life and live a life worth living. Often, when people get what they want, they suddenly realize that it wasn't worth all the anticipation and work—it just doesn't deliver the satisfaction and zest they hoped for and expected. Their willpower is then diminished.

To rev up your willpower you need worthwhile goals; goals that really make you willful. Only godly goals are befitting a godly being—a soul like you.

Ask yourself what inspires your will. When do you feel that you are full of willpower? When you think about it, you will find that that is exactly when you feel the most alive. You feel connected to the life force because you are plugged into the source of all will. Remember your will is really not yours. You are not the source of will, you didn't invent will. You are not free to turn it on and turn it off. As we discussed earlier, if you think your willpower is truly yours then try and stop it for ten seconds. Of course you can't. You have no choice about will. It's not yours to choose. The freedom of choice is *what* you choose. But will flows into you at every moment. So if it is not your will, then whose is it?

Whomever it is that generates your will is the one we refer to as God—the source of all will. It is critical to understand that the more godly your goals, the more the divine will can pour into your life and the more alive and energized you become.[4]

You must get in touch with what you want to do with your life; what makes life worth living. The more what you want is the same as what God wants the more your will actually becomes divine will. You are then connected to the source of everything. You are, so to speak, plugged into *keter*, and you become incredibly resourceful. The more you can align your vision and your plan for yourself and the world with God's vision and plan for you and the world, the greater your willpower and the more resourceful you become.

The Jewish oral tradition declares that whatever the *tzadik*—a person who is connected to the divine—decrees, God fulfills. The mystical dynamic behind that principle is that, in truth, the *tzadik*'s will is already in sync with God's will—his will is God's will.

Torah life is a constant exercise of will. It is a daily fitness plan for the soul. We study Torah to *know* what God wants. We pray in order to *want* what God wants. We obey the commandments in order to *live* what God wants.

The goal of prayer is not to get God to answer your prayers; it's not that God wants what you want. Rather prayer is about you wanting what God wants. The goal of prayer is to pray God's prayer. The sages recorded in the essential prayer of the Jewish liturgy, the *Amidah,* the silent standing prayer, what God wants and therefore what we ask in that prayer is what is truly worth wanting. The more we know, pray, yearn, want, and do what God wants, the more divine willpower pours into us and the more alive and resourceful we become. Divine will generates our very life force and motivates us toward godly heights.

This is powerfully summed up by the simple saying of Rabban Gamliel in *Ethics of the Fathers (Pirkei Avot),* "Make His will your will, so that He will make your will His own."[5]

Rabbi Kook explains:

Man is destined to rise to the recognition of his will, to self-awareness, to the highest perception of happiness in making his own will as the will of his Creator, for his will is none other than his Creator's will. And the more penetrating this recognition, the more it infuses his being.[6]

. . . When desire ascends to the highest planes of consciousness, it becomes clear that no will is separated from the universal will, revealed in all the light of life, in all beings. And the greater this knowledge grows, the more it recognizes the great truth of the ocean of life as it spills into all the rivers of will, collective and individual, the more powerful the influence of the request and its consequences.[7]

When you learn the divine wisdom of the Torah, pray God's prayer and live his commandments you master the "spiritual technology" that empowers you to connect to and channel God's will. In other words, when you want to do what God wants you to do, and you do it as if it is your own will (because it really is—when you are tuned in to your inner self) then your will is as powerful as his own. In reality your will is—at its essence—a stream or ray of divine will.

Imagine yourself as a channel, a water hose with divine will flowing through you. As a flexible hose you can turn yourself in any direction. That's the meaning of free choice. You determine where and into what the will flows. But the direction in which you turn also determines how open the flow is. You could really bend yourself out of shape and, like a kinked water hose, cut the flow off completely. The pressure within you then builds up until, eventually, you burst.

The goal of living a service-driven life is to align yourself with God's will and let it flow powerfully through you, enabling you to accomplish purposeful and meaningful feats. To do this, however, you need a daily exercise plan. If you don't use it, you lose it—just like a muscle. You have to exercise will.

I meet many people who are spiritually out of shape—their will is flabby and lame. What keeps your will strong and fit? How do you exercise your will? By making bold godly choices and committing to act.

Unfortunately, we live in a society that doesn't want to make choices. People want choices made for them. They go to a psychic, so the psychic will tell them what to do. They don't want to take responsibility. If the psychic tells them that this is a good business deal, or a good marriage match, well, good. They don't want to go through the work of deciding what they really want, what their goals are, and they don't take responsibility for their choices. The world is filled with people who are ill from the lack of will. Many people are suffering from weak will. They don't know what they want or what is truly worth wanting or dreaming, planning and committing to.

The root of all life is will. It all starts there. We become resourceful when we reconnect to the all and the source of all by clarifying, wanting, and doing what God—the Great I—wants. When we align our vision with God's vision, our strategy with God's strategy, and when we commit to bringing godly goodness to the world, we enjoy a profound sense of fulfillment.

When we align the stream of our will with God's will, goals, and plan, then all the other *sefirot*—divine powers—will flow abundantly through us. We need to choose to make God's goal our goal, God's plan our plan, God's values our values, God's ways our ways. Otherwise, the divine willpower can't fill us and flow through us. It gets blocked. The more we choose and align ourselves with God's will, purpose, and plan, the more we feel filled with the fullness of God's presence. This is the greatest gift we can give to ourselves.

Chochma

The first thing we should want for our lives is a focus. We should want our lives to be moving toward a clear goal—to be purposeful. To experience ourselves as purposeful, we each need to ask ourselves: "Why on Earth am I here? What am I living for?"

How we answer those questions, how we define our purpose in life determines how we prioritize everything else that we consider important. The quality, vigor, and dynamism of our life flow from the clarity of our purpose.

If my purpose in life is to make a lot of money, then my plan of action flows from there—I may choose to become a thief or an entrepreneur. If my purpose in life is to be world famous, then my plan of action flows from there—I may pursue an acting career or try to do something outrageous enough to get worldwide press coverage.

Now the Torah teaches that our purpose on Earth is to "serve God," which means to serve as a vehicle for making the presence of the Great I manifest on Earth, to materialize spiritual ideals and values in our everyday life. Serving God is not about becoming servile, diminishing ourselves, and bowing before some Super Being "up there." Rather, serving God means becoming godly and channeling the presence of the Great I through what we think, say, and do. Ultimate self-actualization is accomplished through serving God's purpose.

The more we align our individual self with the Universal Self, the more we channel God's presence into our lives and feel fulfilled. The more we sense the presence of the Great I in our life, the more connected we feel to that which is ultimately and forever real.

When you do good for no other purpose other than doing good, then you feel good and feel godlike because God does good for no other purpose than to do good. God, who is complete and is beyond time, surely does not act out of futuristic considerations of gain or personal benefit. When you do good because of the intrinsic value of doing good and not because you want something in return from the recipient or the experience, then you are godlike in the fullest way.

To sum it up in one word—our life's goal is to be holy. This is what God asks of us in the Torah:

You shall be holy, because I, your God, am holy.[8]

All the commandments are guidelines designed to empower us to achieve this goal. But what does it mean exactly? What does it mean to be holy?

The Hebrew for holy is *kadosh*. It is associated with the word *le'hakdish* which means "to dedicate." Therefore, a holy life is a life that is completely devoted and dedicated to being godlike. To be *kadosh* means to give ourselves over entirely to the service of the Great I without any distraction whatsoever. The holy life is a committed life—a life focused with undivided attention on living God's purpose, which is to freely choose to do good for the sake of goodness, to love for the sake of loving.

To do good for the sake of goodness and to give love for the sake of love means for the sake of the here and now without hope of future returns. When our sole purpose is to be godlike—holy—and serve to channel God's goodness and loving presence, then we experience ourselves as purposeful. We feel fulfilled because we are filled to the brim with the One who is already full. We feel like a "someone"—because we experience ourselves as "some" of the One. In truth serving God is self-serving. Since God is the Great I, the Ultimate Self, serving God means manifesting our innermost essence—being completely who we truly are. We are whole and we are holy.

So much of life today is about getting and not giving. Even our giving is often just a way of getting—getting approval, attention, or some kind of return on our investment. That is not love; that is business. That is not about filling our lives with good actions but with transactions.

And so much of life today lacks focus. Our lives are full of distractions. For me, an example of a place that generates the very antithesis of holiness is Times Square. It seems everyone who passes by there is rushing somewhere, talking on the cell phone, texting, shouting, living an ADD lifestyle. In New York City there is an overabundance of stimuli, constant distraction. When I am there I feel it. I am doing this and yet I feel pulled to be doing that. I then experience myself fragmented and scattered.

When I can't stay focused and attuned to God's will to do good and give love then I am unable to be in full service to him as a channel for the presence of the Great I. When I am not whole with what I am doing or when I am not whole with doing it for the one who is whole—the Great I—I cannot feel whole or holy. Holiness means feeling wholeness, being whole with who I am, whole with what I am doing, whole with the moment I am doing it in, whole with whom I am doing it for—whole with doing it for the one who is absolutely whole—God.

To draw the divine power of will into our lives, we need to want to live a life that is purposeful. We need to give our undivided attention and commitment to being godlike—holy—and serve to channel God's goodness and loving presence into whatever we do and to whomever we are with. The holy life is a life committed to being whole and godlike—dedicated and devoted to serving, to revealing the Great I we share and express. We feel whole and complete with what we are doing and whom we are doing it for. We give ourselves completely over to what we are doing in this very moment and we give ourselves completely over to God.

What this means, we learn from Abraham who, when called upon by God, answered simply: *Hineni,* "Here I am." Here I am, completely present and ready to serve you, the Great I—here and now.

I once met a fellow who was completely scattered. While he was talking to me, he was making notes relating to some business matter unrelated to me or our discussion. He was not able to be present. He shared with me that he had dated hundreds of women, but never married because, as he put it, "I'm simply not a good bonder." I could easily see why. "You've got to be present to bond," I told him. "But you're not here. Your body's here, but you're not. You need to be present."

The same is true for our relationship with God. The more we are present, the more we feel the presence of the Great I shining within us. We then experience ourselves as well as all others as a ray of God's light.

To open the channel and let the power of God's will fill you, energize you, and inspire you, you must focus on your purpose in life—to serve God, to make God's will your will, to do good for the pure sake of doing good, to love for the pure sake of loving. You must do this for the simple reason that you know that this is who you are and this is who God is—your will is a stream of his will. How could you not want to do the will of God? It is simply being who you are. You are not doing it to get some benefit from outside of yourself but rather to express that which comes from your innermost self—your godly essence.

Making money is not a purpose in life. Making a living is not making a life. We are making a living, but we have no clue of the life we're making a living for. The value of money is not the number that is written on the piece of paper—the value of money is how it helps us express our real self and become a channel for the divine ideals and values. If our money, property, power, and fame do not serve a higher purpose, a godly purpose, no blessing will come of them.

Becoming mindful of our purpose is referred in the Kabbalah as *chochma* (wisdom). When we tap into the power of *chochma*, we become visionary thinkers with foresight to live daily with the end in mind. And ironically, the end is not in the future but right now—to be holy, to be godlike, choosing to love and do good because that is simply who we are. And being who we are is its own reward.

Bina

What is the difference between a life that is purposeful and a life that is meaningful? Meaning is when we feel we are a means to an end *greater* than ourselves. We don't want to be that end. We don't want to be the selfish center of our lives, which disintegrate when we die. That's a meaningless existence.

Even if our goal is focused beyond ourselves, even if our goal is visionary, we may lack the means to achieve it if we do not have the right plan and strategy. This is where *bina* (insight) comes in.

People who have tapped the divine power of bina enjoy the strategic know-how and means to accomplish their godly goals. Bina is associated with insight because it's one thing to have the wisdom (*chochma*) to know your purpose in general, but it's another thing to really be able to get inside what it is that you have to be doing and get down to the essential and practical daily details necessary to put your purpose into action. You may know that your goal is to be whole and godlike, to become your ultimate self, but you may not know how to actualize your goal.

The Kabbalah teaches that happiness is rooted in the power of bina. One of my teachers once said that "happiness is the certainty of being needed." If you don't feel needed, then you cannot be happy. It's a terrible feeling to feel that no one wants you or cares about you and that your existence doesn't make a difference to anyone.

As a human being, you expect your existence to make a difference. But to whom? The Torah teaches that your life makes a difference to no less than God himself. The Great I is counting on you and me to be a vehicle, a channel, for his presence on Earth— to actualize, through free choice, divine ideals and values in our thoughts, speech, and actions. When you love somebody, is it *your* love you are expressing? Did you create that love, invent it?

Hardly. You're not the source of love, you didn't convince anybody to want love or need love or recognize love, so whose love is it?

In truth, we don't give love or make love—we simply reveal it. Our service is to channel God's love to each other. When I love my wife, I'm actually giving her God's love. When I love my children, I'm giving them God's love.

We are all emissaries of the Great I—assigned to give each other God's love. And if we didn't get love from our mother or father, there's somebody else out there who will give it to us. Be assured that God has an agent appointed to give you love—his love. (But you must also be doing your part by giving love to others.)

God gives us a gift—a meaningful life; the chance to become a means to himself and his purpose. When people live selfish lives, when they live for themselves alone, they become the end (rather than the means) and that is the end of their lives. And they will very possibly even end their lives. But when they feel that their lives are serving some greater end, then they are transported beyond themselves. Living meaningfully is its own reward.

Daat

Once you are connected to the power of purpose (chochma) and the power of meaning (bina), you are able to be decisive and resolute. The union of your dreams (chochma) and strategic plans (bina) generates enormous determination and commitment known as *daat* (knowledge). You know what you want, you know what you have to do, and you know that you can do it.

Daat is considered a lower expression of *keter* and is therefore not counted as a power separate and independent of keter, which is willpower. You are able to tune in to the power of daat only after you have clarified your will using the power of chochma and bina. You then know (via daat) what you want and you take it to heart; you get emotionally charged (via the next three sefirot) and feel poised to put your dreams, plans, and resolutions into action. You are thus able to commit to being faithful to your vision.

On the one hand, if you just have vision (chochma) or see the big picture, and you are charged by the power of the dream but lack detailed strategic planning (bina) then you cannot turn your dreams into reachable goals. On the other hand, if you are on top of your strategic thinking (*bina*) but out of touch with your ultimate dreams and the bigger picture, then you have lost your North Star. You may be making great time in your journey but you are lost at sea. However, when your vision and plans are in focus and in sync with each other, you are blessed with clarity and filled with excitement; you know what you want, and you become infused with a passion to contribute—to do good and give love (which is the next *sefirah—chesed*). However, at this point you are also filled with great trepidation and fear (the counterbalance of *gevurah,* which follows chesed) lest you fail, overshoot, and miss your mark because of your uncontrollable exuberance. Let's examine how that works.

Chesed

Electrified with purpose, meaning, and commitment, you connect to the divine power of *chesed* (kindness) and become energized with a spirit of generosity, kindness, and love. You are charged with an exuberant desire to be helpful well beyond the call of duty. You crave to bountifully extend a helping hand to others and to the world, on God's behalf—with whatever unique talents and gifts he has blessed you with. And you simply love doing God's work.

Each and every one of us has a special godly goodness and a unique way of giving love that we have been destined to channel into the world. You know you have embodied chesed when you can answer the big question: "What good are you?"

What kindness have you come to this world to perform? Are you here to bring beauty via art to the world, or are you here perhaps to bring healing? If you're a doctor, then you serve to channel God's healing power into the world. If you're a teacher then you serve to channel God's wisdom into the world. If you're a garbage man then you serve to bring into the world God's environmental concerns.

Boundless loving and exuberant generosity, however, need to be kept in check lest they overwhelm and harm the giver—this is where the next sefirah comes in.

Gevurah

Gevurah (discipline) provides the right measure of judgment, reserve, and restraint, so chesed doesn't get out of hand.

Maybe you are overextending yourself. Maybe you are putting out more than you can handle and will end up depleted. To counteract the dangers of chesed you must tap the strength of gevurah. To protect yourself from going overboard you must exercise caution.

Gevurah empowers you to safely give of yourself with love and generosity, but also with proper respect for your boundaries and limitations. With gevurah you are able to reign yourself in, pace yourself, and not burn out. Your spontaneous generosity and loving spirit are balanced with discipline. Empowered with gevurah, you become more careful and are duty-bound to follow the rules of genuine love.

When you live by chesed alone, you end up out of control. You become impulsive and obsessive about your giving and overstep your boundaries. Of course, too much *gevurah* would paralyze you. Extreme fear of failure or exaggerated reticence about losing yourself in your passion could eventually lead you to becoming withdrawn, aloof, distant, detached, and unfriendly.

On the Kabbalah's Tree of Life, chesed is linked with chochma because our passions are inspired by our visions and dreams. When you contemplate your visions and vividly see your dreams, your passions intensify. However, gevurah is linked with bina because the power of discipline and self-restraint is rooted in strategic thinking. The more tuned in you are to the power of bina, the more you enhance your power for self-control. You are better able to stick to your plans, play by the rules, and hold fast to its practical details.

Daat is the harmonious intellectual synergy between chochma and bina—the steadfast commitment that translates into a compelling blend of wild dreams (chochma) with calculated design (bina) channeled into a passion for doing good and giving love (chesed) and then tempered by the caution of playing by the requisite rules (gevurah).

Tiferet

Chesed and gevurah are emotional extremes and must be harmonized by the power of *tiferet*. Though translated as "beauty," tiferet is associated with truthfulness and the ability to stay genuine in your giving by regulating its flow. In other words, tiferet is integrity—the power to be truthful and honest with yourself, so that you do not lose yourself. But it is also the power that ensures that your giving is pure and altruistic and not a ploy to really buy someone's favor and get love.

Tiferet is like a faucet that regulates the flow of the hot passion (chesed) with cold, collected restraint (gevurah). To illustrate, let us say that you are a painter and have committed yourself to an art project. If you only operate with chesed, you will paint day and night, indiscriminately splashing paint all over the canvas. However, if you operate with gevurah, you will work five minutes a day making only the tiniest, barely visible strokes on the canvas because you will be paralyzed. This is why you need the power of tiferet as the balancing force, to direct how much paint to apply and how much to withhold.

Now let's take the example of personal relationships. If you are only inspired by chesed, then you will so totally give yourself over to others that you will lose yourself. However, if you are energized by gevurah, then you will become completely withdrawn and hermit-like (indeed, you will not have personal relationships).

Again, tiferet is the trait that keeps you real. It is the ability to be realistic with yourself—who you are and what you are capable of. It balances your passion to give of yourself (chesed) with your restraint and caution to maintain your identity (gevurah). It ensures that you are building a truly beautiful and healthy relationship, where you won't get lost in love. While giving generously, you maintain your personal boundaries. You are expansive while giving of yourself, but without losing yourself because you have the discipline to know when, where, and how much to give.

So if you are giving of yourself in acts of kindness or giving of yourself in love to another person you must be connected to the balancing power of tiferet in order to protect yourself from burnout, remain true to yourself, and ensure that your giving is genuine.

Tiferet is also associated with the power of unconditional love. Because true love is unconditional. I will explain what unconditional love looks like with a story.

One of my students at Isralight was an elderly woman who told me that her son became a drug addict and was institutionalized in a rehab center. One day she received a call from the center telling her that her son left without permission and was probably going to show up at her home. They warned her that this would be the greatest test of how much she really loved her son—if her love was truly unconditional.

"Mrs. Smith, if he comes to your home, you cannot let him in. Otherwise weeks of progress will be destroyed." At that very moment, he knocked on the door. She called out the window, "Who is it?"

"Mom, it's Joey. I got a little time off. They gave me a little vacation because I've been doing so well."

She said, "Joey, I know what's going on; I can't let you in."

"No Mom, you don't understand. I just want to give you a big hug. I just want to spend some time with you, Mom!"

"Joey, I can't let you in."

"Mom! You won't let me into my own home?"

He parked himself on the front steps, ready to wait her out. After a while, it started to rain. He pleaded for her to let him in. She refused and told him to go back to rehab. It was very cold, and the rain turned to sleet. He begged that she throw him a coat. But she refused until he would agree to go back to rehab. There he sat on the front steps in the freezing rain cursing and crying, blaming her for all his problems, telling her what a horrible mother she was and how she didn't love him and never did.

"If you don't let me in I will hate you forever. Wait until I get my hands on you, you wretched witch."

Indeed this was the greatest test of her life and her love. Not only did it test her unconditional love for her son, but also her unconditional love for herself. In other words, this moment revealed whether her love for her son was truly altruistic—because she needed to hold back in the name of love—or just about her need for his love and approval. She had to ask herself if her giving to him all these years was only a way to get him to love her, and therefore it meant she always gave in to him lest his love for her be diminished. Was her giving in his best interest? Was her giving altruistic or was it really a camouflaged desire for getting his love? Could she say no to him even if he really did hate her forever?

This was a moment of truth. She held out. By not letting him into the house, she showed that she was willing to suffer all the embarrassment and personal insults, that her giving was really about unconditional love and not conditional on getting his love back. In other words, true love means giving to another person or withholding from another person based on what is in his or her best interest, without any other consideration in mind. This woman's greatest gift to her son was her holding back from him. The greatest show of her love for him was her willingness to risk his love for her. Because she had the strength to do that, he returned to rehab and was able to complete his treatment.

The Kabbalah teaches that the guiding light of the Torah is rooted in the power of tiferet. Torah brings balance to our daily endeavors and empowers us to stay true to our real inner selves, so that our giving is pure and real. A Torah-based life synthesizes the opposing energies of chesed and gevurah. It guides us in knowing how to cautiously control (gevurah) the flow of our giving (chesed).

The famed composer and teacher Rabbi Shlomo Carlebach was once invited to a college campus to speak to a group of students. Rabbi Carlebach was an overflowing fountain of inspiration and Torah wisdom, so much so that he never needed to prepare his talks. He rarely asked about the topic until he arrived. However, to his surprise, on this occasion he discovered that he was to be part of a debate. "A debate? What's the debate about?" he asked in amazement.

"You're going to be on a panel. There's going to be a Reform rabbi, a Conservative rabbi, and an Orthodox rabbi—you. And the topic for the debate is: Did God give the Torah at Sinai?"

Rabbi Carlebach was given the podium first—the organizers clearly assumed that he would maintain that God did give the Torah at Sinai and then the other rabbis would shoot down his arguments. But Rabbi Carlebach said, "Before I can even talk about whether the Torah is from God, I need to talk about how much we need a Torah from God. Because if we don't think we need a Torah from God, it doesn't really matter if there is a Torah from God."

"You know, friends," he continued, "we're the only creatures in the world who need guidance. It's unbelievable. Animals, they know exactly who they are and what to do. They're so clever. But we humans are so confused and can so easily think we are someone that we are not. I have never seen a dog pretending to be a goldfish but there are lots of people trying to be who they are not. Have you ever seen an animal being born? I remember I was with my children on a kibbutz and I saw with my own eyes that after a calf is born, within minutes it stands up. It's unbelievable. If we were Martians from another planet, and we landed on the planet Earth and saw a woman give birth to a baby and a cow give birth to a calf, who would we think is the superior being on Earth? The cow, for sure. We're the only creatures in the world who need guidance. So why don't we look for guidance?"

The guidance of the Torah empowers us to balance our passions with our cautions and reservations so that we can stay true to ourselves and ensure our loving is unconditional—regardless of what others think of us. The Torah teaches how to negotiate and navigate the balance between how much to give and how much to hold back.

Once we master our choices to do good and give love—via chesed, gevurah, and tiferet—we must master the powers (the next three sefirot) that help us adjust ourselves to fit the needs and limitations of the various situations we find ourselves in.

Netzach, Hod, Yesod

Netzach means to be victorious, to conquer. It is also translated as eternity, but in the context of choosing to do good and give love it refers to undying effort, endurance, permanence, determination, tenacity, and persistence in spite of all obstacles and discouragements. It's the power to overcome barriers and make things happen. People who embody netzach are forward-thinking, success-minded achievers. They always see more that still needs to be done—more territory to conquer. They always have their foot on the gas pedal.

The word *netzach* is also associated with the Hebrew word *minazayach*—a conductor of a symphony, a director of a project; in other words, someone who takes control. On the Kabbalah's Tree of Life, netzach is linked with chesed because extreme giving creates dependence and allows for the control of others.

Hod is associated with the Hebrew word *l'hodot* which means to be thankful and grateful. It also means to acknowledge and admit. Hod, therefore, is the power to acknowledge and accept what cannot be changed.

In contrast to people who embody netzach, who always see how much more there is to conquer, hod-oriented people gratefully acknowledge how far they have come. If netzach is about making things happen and moving upward and onward to overcome obstacles and conquer more and more territory, hod is about letting go, accepting the limitations of what cannot be changed, letting things happen, and being thankful for whatever the outcome happens to be.

Hod is the ability to take directions—that is why when God commanded Moses to appoint judges. He instructed Moses to extend his hod to them because they needed the ability of hod to submit to God's authority, accept the direction of God's laws, and make decisions like Moses. Hod, therefore, is the power to surrender, submit, retreat, yield, comply, and acquiesce. People who embody hod are open-minded; they are adaptable to the developing needs of a situation.

A hod-oriented person, without the counterbalance of netzach, can become meek, timid, passive, and even lazy. A netzach-oriented person without the counterbalance of hod will be unyielding, stubborn, overbearing, overpowering, aggressive, and even hostile.

How do netzach and hod look in action? Here is an illustration:

If you are a painter, you will have to take into consideration not only what you want to paint (chochma and bina) and not just what you are capable of painting (chesed, gevurah, tiferet), but also what is realistically possible. You will need to interface with given factors. How much paint do you have? What's the size of the available canvas? What do time, space, and budget allow? Netzach urges you to drive regardless of the limitations; its motto is, "We shall overcome!" Hod would have you give up before you even start, so conscious it makes you of your obstacles. This is why netzach and hod operate best with the balancing factor of yesod.

Yesod means "foundation"—like the foundation of a building that anchors the structure in the ground. In other words, *yesod* is what ensures that what you are doing is grounded in reality.

Yesod is the power of flexibility and responsibility—the ability to respond to the hard facts on the ground and the flexibility to then properly adjust yourself to that reality. You are not just living in your own world, oblivious to the borders and obstacles, stubbornly moving forward (that would be extreme netzach), and you are also not allowing your awareness of the limitations paralyze you and give up hope (that would be extreme hod). Thanks to yesod (which integrates netzach and hod) you are able to move forward responsibly with cautious confidence, to roll with the punches. You know how much you can stretch your borders and make things happen and when to let up before they break.

Yesod is also associated with justice because it justifies your ideals within the confines of what's real so you are on target. Yesod is also identified with the power to make peace as it is the ability to negotiate a possible relationship between the ideal and the real, between what you want to do and what is possible and practical, between what you have to give and what the project needs.

Now let's look at netzach, hod, yesod in terms of personal relationships.

Remember, the powers of chesed, gevurah, and tiferet enable you to give to others in a way that is truly giving and not a disguised form of taking. Tiferet ensures that you are realistic about yourself and that you give with integrity; that you stay true to the real inner you and do not get lost in the relationship. Now, netzach, hod, and yesod guide you in considering how much your partner is able to receive.

Everybody knows that love is give and take. But you also have to make sure that your "give" fits the other's "take." Otherwise, there is no peace in the relationship, just frustration. Your partner will either feel unfulfilled or overwhelmed. He or she will either feel you are too hod-oriented (reserved, removed, aloof, withdrawn, evasive, submissive, and passive), or too netzach-oriented (domineering, aggressive, invasive, and overbearing).

Remember that some of this depends on the person's perspective—how you come across to your partner. You might think you are being true to your gevurah, respectful of your partner's personal boundaries, keeping the borders clear, holding back from any assumptions and maintaining self-control. But to your partner, from his or her perspective, you might be coming across as someone who is totally hod—passive, submissive, aloof, and so forth. Or, you may have thought that you were relating with chesed—giving generously, showing initiative, offering intimacy. But to your partner, the way you are coming across might look like netzach—controlling, forceful, aggressive, overwhelming, and so on. Therefore, you need to consider how you are coming across—in action as well as in communication. You need to accord your message to what your partner is able to receive and to hear. If it's too much, you will blow her away, but if not enough, you will simply bore him.

Another balancing function of yesod is the ability to compromise, to make peace. Unlike truth, which is the way it is, peace is how to bend and come together. If you hold to your truth, there may not be room for connection. Therefore, you want to be true to yourself (tiferet), yet at peace with others (yesod).

When you tap the power of yesod you are realistic, responsible, flexible, cooperative, coordinated, down-to-earth, grounded, balanced, stable, and peaceful.

Yesod as Culminating Power

Yesod, however, is more than just the coordinating power of netzach and hod—it is really the collecting point of all the divine energies from keter all the way down to hod. It is the culmination of the entire process of serving the Great I by choosing to do good and give love. All the divine powers become synthesized together and ready to be given over to the recipient, which is referred to in Kabbalah as *malchut*—the "kingdom."

The kingdom represents the person or the project we are investing in, whoever or whatever we are building, enhancing, helping, loving, and caring for. Therefore, when you are connected to yesod—which is only possible once you have served to channel all the other powers—you feel whole and alive because you are useful and productive, blessed because you are successful, and joyful that all of the godly attributes are integrated within you.

Yesod is also associated with *chen*—grace or charisma. The Kabbalah teaches that Joseph was the archetypical model of yesod and that he radiated chen. Everybody loved Joseph (except his brothers), including the master of the house in which he was a slave and later even the pharaoh of Egypt.

What did the pharaoh see in Joseph? He saw that Joseph was connected to God. After Joseph explained the pharaoh's troubling dreams, the pharaoh said: "Can another one like this be found, a man who has God's spirit in him?"[9]

When you live in full service of the Great I and you embody the presence of God in you, then people see the talents and gifts you bear as divine. You are masterful—filled with the presence of the Master. You live as an agent of the Great I, representing God and doing his work. In fact the word *charisma* comes from the Greek language and means "divine gift or favor." When you embody all the divine powers and serve to channel God's presence into the world, you will surely exude charisma and grace. People will be drawn to you and trust you.

There is really only one road to success in life and only for this purpose have we been created—to serve the Great I by freely choosing to do good and give love. We are here on Earth to successfully channel divine creativity and love into whatever we do and whoever we are with. Our goal is to infuse the presence of the Great I into all actions and all relationships. This is the secret to true success because when we are doing what we were created for, we bring blessing to every deed and every relationship.

However, when we fail in our mission, or refuse it, we are like a vending machine that's "out of service." Then no matter how busy we are, inside we feel empty and useless. To feel useless is hell but to feel divinely useful is heaven on Earth.

God has given every single one of us a special talent and a divine mission. God blessed me with the gift of gab. I did nothing for this. I was doing theatrical plays when I was a kid and I always got the best part because I had no problem speaking up in front of a lot of people. I did nothing for this—it was just a God-given gift. When I was a kid, I thought I'd be an actor, but when I got older I decided to be a rabbi.

How did I make that decision? A number of professions use the gift of gab in various ways. But, since I knew inside myself that God blessed me with the ability to communicate, I knew that I had to communicate whatever God wanted me to. How could I communicate junk? As a rabbi, I feel so divinely useful when I teach. To be able to use my talents to serve God—to do good by inspiring people to love life, love themselves, and love others—is for me, bliss.

Every single one of us has a talent. There's absolutely no question about that. The only question is what we do with it. How are we going to use it to serve the Great I?

Consider how you are channeling the ten sefirot of Divine Presence into this world. Are you aware of your divine purpose (chochma) and divine meaning (bina)? Have you aligned your vision for yourself with God's vision for you (chochma), your plans with God's plans (bina)? Are you decisive and committed (daat)? Are you passionately doing good and giving love? Are you contributing to the world—making it a better place, a sanctuary for God's love and goodness? Are you helping people live better, love deeper, and be happier (chesed)? Are you disciplined; careful to do it right? Are you sticking to God's plan and playing by his rules (gevurah)? Are you doing it with integrity? Are you realistic about yourself, staying true to who you are? Is your love true and unconditional (tiferet)? Are you determined and persistent (netzach)? Are you able to accept insurmountable limitations, let go and let it happen, and be thankful for whatever the outcome (hod)? Are you able to respond to the hard facts on the ground and be flexible, properly adjusting yourself to the realities of the project or the person (yesod)?

If you can answer all these questions with a resounding yes, then you are plugged in to the divine. You are truly alive and blessed; successful and joyful. Every fiber of your being is alive here and now, exuding godliness. You are a living example of the Torah's declaration:

> You who are bonded with the Lord, your God, are alive, totally, today.[10]

This is what Torah promises us. This is what its wisdom and ways deliver.

Here's a prayer worth saying every morning when you get up: "Please God, use me. Let me live in sweet service of you, the Great I. Let me be your glove to do your work on Earth—to freely choose to do good and give your love to all."

Malchut

Sometimes the greatest goodness you can do for others is to let others do good for you. Sometimes the greatest way of giving love is to let others give love to you. In order to be complete in your service of the Great I, you must master the art of receptivity.

Some people know how to love but do not know how to be loved. *Malchut* is associated with humility because that's what it takes to be receptive to the goodness and love of others. To be receptive you must humbly acknowledge the empty places within yourself that need to be filled by others.

I had a friend who was totally shocked when his wife suddenly asked for a divorce. It seemed to come out of nowhere. He was always so kind and loving to her. There was simply nothing he would not have done for his wife, so intense was his passion for her. Unfortunately, there was something that he never did for his wife. There was a goodness that he unknowingly withheld from her all the years of their marriage. Although he regularly showered her with gifts, there was one gift he never gave her and that was the gift of letting her give to him. Although he felt so one with her and could not fathom living without her, she did not feel as connected to him.

We feel connected to the people we give to, much more so than to those from whom we receive. Children and parents are a great example of this—the parents give so much to their children, who cannot reciprocate, and invariably parents are much more invested in their children than vice versa. Simply being the recipient of love cannot create the same kind of bond of attachment.

To be a player in God's drama of doing good and giving love, we must give, but we must also give others the opportunity to give to us; to love us. And of course the greatest gift we give to others and receive from others is the ability to discover our unique mission in life so that we can serve the Great I. To empower and to be empowered with visionary and strategic thinking (chochma and bina), decisiveness (daat), passionate giving (chesed), cautious restraint (gevurah), integrity (tiferet), persistence (netzach), adaptability and compliance (hod), responsibility and flexibility (yesod), and receptiveness and humility (malchut).

Summary

It takes more that just an attitude for the service-driven life to become a path to personal fulfillment. We need a daily spiritual fitness plan to get our souls in shape and get to work. To access our godly greatness and make I-contact we need to learn how to align our individual self with the Universal Self and channel God's presence into everything we think, say, and do. To accomplish this we must align our will, vision, and plans for ourselves and the world with God's will (keter), vision (chochma), and plans (bina). We must be decisive and committed (daat) to passionately helping people to live better, love deeper, and be happier (chesed). But we must also be disciplined about it, sticking to God's plan and playing by his rules (gevurah). This, however, needs to be done with integrity (tiferet) and persistence (netzach), and yet with acceptance of insurmountable limitations: letting go and being thankful for whatever the outcome (hod). All this requires flexibility—the ability to adjust to the realities of the project or the person (yesod). And last but not least we must be willing and able to allow others to help us and humbly receive from them (malchut).

To put our plan into action we must always stay focused on our godly goal. God asks of us: *You shall be holy, because I, your God, am holy.* Start each day with this end in mind. A holy life is life focused with undivided attention on living God's purpose—to love and do good for their own sake without hopes for future returns. God, who is complete and beyond time, does not act out of futuristic considerations of benefit or personal gain. Embodying this truth we become godlike in the fullest way. We become filled with the fullness of God's presence; every fiber of our being comes alive here and now exuding godliness.

As exciting and promising as all this sounds there is one last point that we must take to heart and never forget.

10

Endless Journey, Endless Joy

VERY OFTEN RELIGION is presented as offering the secret to ultimate happiness. I have heard religious leaders try to entice people toward a religious lifestyle promising them that through their synagogue or their church, all will find happiness and bliss.

This approach is really no different than any other marketing strategy. People want to be happy and are looking for the magic formula. Marketers know this, and they bombard us daily with promises for a better life: "Blondes have more fun," or "Lose weight and feel great" or "Things go better with Coke." People think that all they need is *the more* and *the right*. If only I had more hair, more muscle, more money, and so on. If only I had the right boyfriend/girlfriend, the right job, the right apartment, and so forth. People are hoping to find a quick and easy formula for happiness. They want to just add water and stir. They want to pop their problems into a microwave and have happiness ready in seconds.

And there are religious leaders who make that very promise. They claim that all you have to do is believe. All you have to do is follow the word of God and you've got it made. God will take care of you, and your life will be blessed with bliss.

I agree with them that faith, study, and practice are a lot better products to buy than a new car, nicer clothing, or more expensive perfume. But I do not agree that religion is going to give anyone a quick fix. Or that religion is going to put anyone on easy street.

Did Abraham have an easy life? Hardly. The Torah teaches us that Abraham was challenged with ten difficult tests. Jacob had an even more troubling life than Abraham. For years he lived as a fugitive running from his brother who sought to kill him. His daughter was raped. His wife died while giving birth. Unbeknownst to him, Jacob's sons sold their younger brother Joseph as a slave, and Jacob mourned his loss for years until he was finally reunited with Joseph. Jacob did not have a blissful life.

The life of David, who authored many of the psalms, was definitely not a merry-go-round either. He, too, was a fugitive, running from King Saul who was determined to kill him. Later on in his life, when he became king, his own son tried to kill him in an attempt to usurp the throne. Many of the psalms David wrote captured the depth of a person who struggled with the most trying of times. Millions of people for thousands of years have turned to the psalms in their most painful moments, finding solace in the words of a man who was able to express their pain, fears, and hopes.

The general history of the Jewish people has certainly not been a barrel of laughs. Has any other nation on Earth suffered as much as the Jews? The Jewish people have throughout their history experienced the gamut of tragedy, cruelty, and pain. Highlights include two hundred and ten years of slavery in Egypt, being burned and slaughtered during the Inquisition, pillaged and raped during regular pogroms in Russia and Eastern Europe, and gassed by the millions in the Holocaust. And yet the Torah refers to the Jewish people as the chosen people. They are described as the firstborn of God and a treasured nation.

The "Soul-ution"

People are looking for happiness in all the wrong places. And they will never find it because happiness is not something you find outside; it lies within—within your soul.

You cannot *find* happiness. Happiness does not just happen; rather, you have to learn to *be* happy in whatever is happening.

A service-driven life does not offer any dispensations from the challenges of life. It does not promise an easy life; it promises a purposeful and meaningful life. It does not offer an instant solution to sadness but it does offer a "soul-ution" to sadness and the secret to happiness. Service empowers us to be a soul and enables us to make I-contact with the Soul of souls, in service of our Ultimate Self, God.

I have seen plenty of people jump into a Judaism—learning its wisdom and following its laws—and yet they are not happy. But that is because they thought it was a quick fix and the road to bliss. These people are only studying and practicing the Torah, but they are not immersed it. They may keep Shabbat, but they are not celebrating Shabbat. They might be observing the *mitzvot* (commandments), but they are not living the mitzvot. These people are religious and yet unhappy because they are not willing to really embrace the challenges of life and do the inner soul work that the Torah is expecting and guiding us to live. They have not turned their lives into a daily service of God. They have lost themselves in the laws rather than finding themselves in God.

Life lived in accordance with the Torah is likened to a song. To make music you need to be more than just a technician; you need to be a musician. You have to play the song with more than just your fingers. You have to play it with your soul. And when you do you experience the Great Musician playing the song through you.

Ironically, the service-driven life, while leading us to true happiness, makes us more susceptible to sadness. This is the meaning of King Solomon's wise words recorded in the Book of Ecclesiastes: "With a lot of wisdom comes a lot of heartache. The greater your knowledge, the greater your pain."[1] In other words, ignorance is bliss. However, a true pursuit of a conscious and soulful life actually brings you greater challenges and more sadness then before you even embarked on the journey. This is because the more conscious we become of our soul's desire to serve and make I-contact with the Great I, the more sadness we feel over the lack of that service and connection. There is a deep inner pain and sadness in a soul who feels far from God, who is unfulfilled in the desire to bond with God and operate from a place of inner freedom in service of the Great I.

Our soul naturally longs to bond with God, as in the words of the Book of Psalms: "As a deer yearns for streams of water, so my soul yearns for You, O God."[2] When we feel this inner sadness and know that something is missing in our life, we often turn to the superficial things. We mistakenly think that it must be that new car or new job that we are missing. But none of it satisfies. It only pains our soul. What pains the soul most is the lack of freedom. The soul wants the freedom to bond completely with God and to freely express itself as a ray and manifestation of the Great I.

When we feel disconnected from the Great I, we feel alienated, suppressed, oppressed, and stifled from being the unique divine channel we are meant to be. Our deepest desire is to freely express the Great I in the special way that each of us can. We want a life that is noble, elevated, and refined. We yearn to radiate the light of God—the light of love, goodness, compassion, and truth.

Therefore, when you allow yourself to hear the inner voice of your soul's yearning for spiritual greatness, you may feel much sadness. It may then seem hopeless when you realize that the more you awaken to your soul's desire for God, the sadder and the more discontented you will be. But the path to true happiness is to embrace your soul's sadness and discontentment. The sadness and discontentment of the soul is actually the very material from which the soul makes joyous music.

If you did not feel this sadness, then you would be doomed to death. If you reach a point where you are no longer longing for God in your life, then you have no life anymore.

It takes maturity and courage to be willing to acknowledge and feel the pain of the soul that is pining for God. Most of us think there is something wrong with us if we are unhappy. We feel guilty over our discontent and look for a painkiller. But in truth, this pain is the source of great pleasure. When we come to understand the true meaning of this sadness, we are happy. In fact, we realize that our sadness is a sure sign of our spiritual greatness and wellness because it comes from a deep yearning to serve and feel close to God. Then we discover that, in a paradoxical way, there is great joy in this kind of sadness—it is invigorating and motivating.

When we awaken to our thirst for God, we discover that that thirst can never be quenched because we can never be completely united with God. There is always the possibility for more spiritual growth and a deeper connection. Mysteriously, in the spiritual life the more full we feel, the more empty we feel. The more connected we feel to the Great I, the more disconnected we feel because we realize how much more connected we could be. Just as soon as we feel whole with God, we feel a huge hole in life that is missing the Ultimate Self. In the spiritual life to feel whole means to be constantly filling that hole with more and more communion with God. And the more we fill it, the bigger it gets.

If all we really want out of life is Calvin Klein jeans, tickets to a Madonna concert, and a Ferrari to drive, then it is really no big deal if we don't get what we want. None of these leaves a gaping hole in our soul if we don't get it. We are not missing much because we are not asking for much. In addition, such desires can be fulfilled. But when we tap into the soul's desire and yearning for a connection to God, then what we are really asking for is to connect with the One who is infinite, who is endless. The thirst for God can never be quenched, because it is an endless thirst for the Endless One.

Ironically, once we tap in and tune in to the yearning of our soul we actually end up feeling sadder. In other words the greater our spiritual consciousness and our desire for God, the sadder we feel. But in truth, the secret to true happiness lies precisely in the depth of this sadness of the soul. The Book of Psalms advises: "Rejoice in your heart—you who seek God."[3] It does not say "you who *find* God." Why? Because we will never find God. In fact, if God could be found then we would be eternally depressed.

Fortunately the soul's desire for God can never be fulfilled. The soul's joy is always to be seeking God but never quite finding God. This guarantees that the journey and adventure of love will never end. There is so much joy in the sadness of a soul that is lovesick for God. As soon as we feel close we feel far and thankfully the journey goes on forever. In other words, as soon as we think we have found love, we have actually lost it because love is not a thing we can acquire or accomplish, but an endless journey we take.

The miracle of love and the beauty of love is that there is no end to the depth of love. We can love each other more and more every day. Love is not a destiny; it is a journey—an endless journey.

When Moses encountered the burning bush that miraculously was not consumed and heard the voice of God, he turned away so as not to look. He was afraid he had found God and that his spiritual journey and search was over. True seekers never want to find God, they want to feel that they are always finding God, and there is always more to find.

The prophets teach that in the future there will be a hunger and thirst in the world, not for bread and water, but for God. When you are hungry for bread you feel empty but when you are hungry for God you feel full. The soul is satiated by its hunger for God. There is so much joy in the anticipation of getting forever closer and closer to our Endless Self.

Therefore, when we hear the voice of our soul, our true self, yearning to connect with God, the Great I, we experience intense sadness. However, when we embrace that sadness, we are indeed on the road to happiness.

The Role of Sadness

To me this truth was a huge revelation. I used to think that the more I could tune in to my soul and my true inner desires then the happier I would be. I too expected that once I lived by the word of God and made it the center of my life's focus, I would be happy as a lark. But just the opposite happened. I suddenly felt sadder than I ever felt before in my carefree secular life.

One night my wife, Chana, and I were walking downtown on

our way to a class. All along the street were pubs, bars, and discos. There was merriment in the air. Music was blaring from all sides. People were drinking, eating, laughing, dancing, and having a great time. Everyone seemed so happy. So I asked my wife, "What do you think about this? People say that if a person has the Torah in her life then she is really happy. Do you think that is true? Do we not meet people that seem to be very happy that are not living the Torah, people who are very secular and very materialistic? There seems to be a lot of people who are happy to just party every night, make lots of money, and enjoy their sex life. Is it correct to say that they are not happy?"

Chana responded, "It all depends on the level of consciousness that a person has. If a person doesn't have a very high level of spiritual awareness, well then they are very happy with very little." In other words if a person is struggling with issues like "Am I a good person?" "What more can I do to better the world?" "Is my life purposeful and meaningful?" "How can I feel more connected to God?" then they have much discontent and sadness in their lives.

Essentially, successful materialists can—at best—only be content but not truly happy. And unless they succeed in completely strangling their soul, they are heading for depression. Because the soul will be knocking at them from within, spoiling their contentment. To be happy they will need to embrace the joy that is hidden in the sadness of their soul yearning for God.

Don't let looks fool you. When you see a dog wagging his tail gobbling away his food, he seems very happy, and we can understand why because his request for food has been satisfied. But then all he wanted was a can of Alpo and some water. His expectations are not high nor his desires great. His soul is not struggling with annoying questions about meaning and spiritual growth. He is not pained by the evil and cruelty in the world unless it personally affects him. It is easy to make an animal happy, but the more developed our spiritual consciousness the greater our potential for sadness because what we yearn for is more than just to wag our tails—we want to set our soul free to serve and soar toward endless heights. Therefore, the more spiritually evolved a person becomes the more apt they are to be sad.

My neighbors were doing renovations in their home so they asked me if I could take care of their aquarium. It was quite a spiritual experience to see these fish daily. Every day I would look at them and say, "Thank God I am not a fish." There was one big ugly fish that just lay there on the bottom and hardly moved. His job and joy was to eat the excrement of all the other fish. These fish looked very happy and content. Well, why not? They don't struggle with the annoying questions about the purpose and meaning of their lives. Every day I would look at those poor little happy fish, and I felt happy that I was sad—that I was a soul and that I could hear the sadness of my soul and happily search for God, longing for the Great I.

Don't run away from the sadness of your soul. It is the motor that propels you forward in your spiritual journey. It is the source of great inspiration and creativity.

Now I have to admit that I once met an actor who told me that his acting teacher advised him never to go to therapy because neurosis is the source of creativity and the secret to becoming a great actor. I wouldn't go so far and say, "Stay neurotic, nuts, and compulsive because that is what inspires your creativity." Only egos get neurotic and that happens because they are not willing to hear the sadness of the soul, inspiring them to embark on the joyous endless journey toward our Endless Self—God.

At first, this may not be clear. When you first embark on the service-focused journey toward I-contact, you will not feel instant bliss. You may find that before you were sad because you were missing a Ferrari, but now you are sad because you are missing God. When you get to this point, as scary as it feels, don't run away from the sadness, run into it and the gateways to happiness will be flung open.

Sadness versus Depression

We get depressed not because we don't know how to be happy, but because we don't know how to be sad. When we deny the sadness of our soul and run from its painful longing for meaning, service, and God, that is when we get depressed. We need to learn how to be sad before we can be happy, otherwise we are on the road to depression.

People frantically run from the sadness of their soul seeking happiness. Most forms of fun, entertainment, and amusement are really painkillers. They are part of the great escape from the sadness of the soul. When you go to a doctor with something hurting you, he can give you an aspirin to stop the pain. If the pain is too great for aspirin, then he can give you codeine. But even though you don't feel the pain you are still not healthy.

A truly healthy soul is one who is lovesick for God. But people look for painkillers to stop the pain and drown out the sadness of their soul, which is aching for God. Because they are afraid to be sad, they run for distractions.

I know this from experience. For years I ran from the sadness of my soul. I threw myself into comedy and rock 'n' roll. They were my religion. I once heard a comedian say that as long as you keep laughing, you will never get an ulcer. So that's what I did. And he was right. I didn't get an ulcer. I got a hernia instead. I adopted as my philosophy for life the lyrics of a popular song at the time by Dobie Gray about freeing my soul, getting lost in rock and roll and drifting away.

I recall one rock album I especially loved that had on the cover the following advice: "For best results play at full blast!" But what were the results that I was seeking? I wanted enough noise and distraction in my life to drown out my crying soul. But the louder the music, the louder my soul cried out. So the louder I turned up the music.

People confuse painlessness with happiness. But the key to happiness is to embrace the sadness of the soul craving for purpose and meaning, yearning God. Because within this sadness is the greatest happiness.

The soul cries for purpose and meaning. We long for God. We long to belong to the One who is beyond and yet mysteriously manifest within ourselves. We want to be part of a greater picture and we want to feel that we are playing a role serving a greater purpose, the Greater Self. But most people run from this sadness rather than stop and listen carefully. Rather than make music out of the soul's sadness they turn up the volume on their CD player.

A story is told of a king who upon waking in the morning was always serenaded by a musical quartet. While eating he was entertained by the court jester. Every night he threw a royal ball and danced with the fairest of maidens into the night. The king was constantly bombarded with stimulus to keep him happy. Otherwise in just one quiet moment without the joker and the music playing he would suddenly hear his crying soul and not be able to bear it.

This is the strategy of most people. They try to fill their lives with distractions to protect themselves from feeling the emptiness and sadness in their soul. But this kind of happiness is truly sad because this kind of fulfillment is truly empty. You can't *get* happy—you have to *be* happy, but first you have to be willing to be sad. The gateway to happiness is the sadness of the soul.

The secret to fulfillment and happiness is to embrace the emptiness and the sadness of the soul and give voice to your soul's yearning to make I-contact with our Endless I—God.

If you just run for fun then you're done. Depression doesn't descend upon us because we are not able to be happy, but because we are not willing to be sad. Before a depressed person can be happy, he or she must first be sad.

A drug addict who has beaten his addiction has still not solved his problem; rather, he has just succeeded in getting rid of that which distracted him from dealing with the real problems that he was running from. Like the old African adage says: "You can run away from that which is running behind you, but not that which is running inside you." Drugs, alcohol, eating disorders are not problems—they are really cover-ups for problems. Once you kick the habit, the real work starts. Once you kick the habit, don't be surprised if you are depressed. But the first step out of that depression is to acknowledge and feel the sadness of your soul longing for God. The first step to spiritual health is to be lovesick for God.

Fun versus Happiness

What is the difference between having fun and being happy?

Happiness is not dependent on an event or something that you have, it is an inner state of being that does not happen to you but that you must achieve. Happiness is not a happening, it is a choice—a choice to work at achieving happiness. Therefore you can always be happy, regardless of the events that are happening around you. And as explained above, we as a soul are the happiest when we sadly long for God and use that sadness to motivate us to greater service.

Fun is an event; it does not affect your inner being. It is an occurrence that happens from time to time. It would be great if we were having fun while being happy. But life sometimes is not fun. It may even be very bitter and painful. However, even in those times, we can be happy. Fun is an occasional happening and even if you could have fun every day, it would not make you happy.

The Torah teaches that the way to happiness is to allow the sadness of your soul to motivate you to apply your intelligence and skills to do the will of God, bring his goodness into the world and spread his love. When your soul is in harmony with the whole divine symphony of life then it feels a deep happiness while sadly longing for even more harmony. Then, when you experience painful events, your inner constant state of happiness is untouched. Therefore, even if you should encounter great suffering, you are still in a state of inner happiness. But if you turn away from God, you choose a life of dissonance. You are not interested in coordinating your actions with God's vision, plan, and ways. Even if you are having fun daily, none of it affects your inner self that is actually broken and depressed.

You can *have* fun but you can only *be* happy.

The Value of Happiness

We read in the Book of Psalms that a "man is born a wild donkey."[4] Our task is to transform our wild drives into uniquely human powers by properly nurturing and directing them toward achieving the ideals for which they were created. Otherwise rather than bringing us blessing, these drives will destroy us.

Some people may look at these drives in their primitive and gross form and think that they should be uprooted. But that approach will never succeed. Others may decide that since these drives are intrinsic to human nature, then they should simply be allowed free rein and expression. This attitude is irresponsible and dangerous. The Torah teaches us that everything that comes from God has a divine reason behind it, and we must harness the power of these drives and elevate them toward their higher intended purpose.

Urges, inclinations, and tendencies are called in Hebrew *netiot*. This same word also means "young saplings." Therefore, the successful fruition of these young saplings—our primitive urges— is that they be planted in the right ground to bear delicious and nourishing fruits. This is one of the goals of Gods' commandments—to direct and harness man's wild, animalistic drives and use them to serve a divine purpose, as befits the greatness of a human being created in the image of God.

It is basic human nature to want to be happy. However, the urge for happiness in its primitive form can be satisfied through lusts and cravings. We feel good when we eat a steak, drink wine, win a game, indulge in sex. But transient pleasures do not fulfill our soul. Ultimately the life of lust leaves our inner self empty and depressed. Of course, this does not mean we should give up our hopes for happiness. We just have to realize that deep and lasting happiness comes from serving God's purpose to make manifest in this world divine ideals and values. When we do good, we feel good and become godly. Only good, loving, and meaningful acts can bring us real happiness.

This is what King Solomon is referring to in the Book of

Ecclesiastes when he praises happiness and yet also questions its value. He is referring to these two types of happiness. The happiness derived from doing good deeds is the kind that is praiseworthy. However when happiness comes from any other source it is worthless in his opinion.

When we satisfy our lusts then our egos and bodies are fulfilled. But even so lust has a short life. As soon as a lust is fulfilled it dies. It is only the pleasures of the soul that last forever. This is what the psalmist means when he says, "I will rejoice in God."[5] In other words, when I make God the context of my life and his service my frame of reference, then I am happy.

The Talmud teaches that the indwelling presence of God—called the *Shechina*—cannot inspire a person who is lazy, depressed, or flippant. The *Shechina* inspires only those who are happy doing a good deed and living God's word.

At such times we experience the eternal magnificence of our soul because we see ourselves as part of the divine universal soul that is manifest in all of creation, giving it life and directing it toward its ultimate purpose. This is the meaning of the statement in the Book of Psalms, "God, You make me happy in all that You do, I will sing joyfully about the works of your hands."[6]

In other words, we feel truly happy when we experience whatever we are doing as the doings of God—that God is actually working through us, and we are divine instruments. The artist is in ecstasy when he no longer feels that he is the painter but rather the paintbrush in the hand of the One and Only True Artist.

The German philosopher Friedrich Nietzsche once said, "Unless you feel that an infinite whole is working through you, your life has no meaning." Torah would add that your life also has no real happiness.

We are inspired by the *Shechina* and achieve true happiness when we perceive ourselves as participating in the universal spirit and partaking in the power of God. There is profound joy in experiencing ourselves serving as God's tools bringing divine love and goodness to the world.

Therefore when you are connected to God and experiencing I-contact with the Great I, you feel energized by the divine spirit that is inherent in all of creation. You feel vibrant, alive, and happy—not sluggish, lazy, or depressed. When the *Shechina* inspires your actions, you are directed and not flippant. When you speak, your words are filled with meaningful content, not mundane chatter.

But if you are not connected, then you have to "fake it till you make it." Jump out of bed, even though you don't feel like it. Meditate and contemplate the awesome spirit of life that is not yours but God's. Envision yourself as part of the great divine light that is manifest in this miraculous universe. Then go out and love, do good, and you will feel good and you feel God.

It is not enough to just be busy. You have to be focused to be effective. Sure you could feel happy if you put on some funky music and start to boogie, but that will not bring your soul into contact with the *Shechina*. It won't deliver the real happiness that lasts. Yes, you could go see a hysterically funny comedy and laugh your guts out. But no movie runs forever. You could go play some basketball, work up a good sweat. But even if you win the game, you may still feel like a loser. Instead, engage a friend in a meaningful conversation, share words of wisdom, do a good deed, visit the sick, give charity to the poor, comfort the mourner, help out at an orphanage, volunteer at a shelter for the homeless or a soup kitchen, cheer up the downtrodden, offer a kind word and friendly smile. The list is endless, the service is endless, the journey is endless and so is the joy. Thank God.

The Book of Psalms states, "In Him our hearts find joy"[7] and "I will find joy in the LORD."[8] When we realize that God is the all-embracing context of our lives and live in tandem with that truth we are filled with profound and sacred joy.

Summary

The service-driven life does not offer us instant happiness. In fact, the more conscious we are of our desire to serve and connect with the Great I the more sadness we feel over the lack of an even greater connection. Paradoxically, the secret to true happiness lies precisely in the depth of this sadness of the soul. We get depressed not because we don't know how to be happy, but because we don't know how to be sad; because we deny the sadness of our soul and run from its painful longing for meaning and God. The key to happiness is to embrace the sadness of the soul craving for God and godly purpose because it is actually the very motor that propels us forward in our spiritual journey, invigorating and motivating us to bring greater goodness and show greater love. The Book of Psalms advises: "Rejoice in your heart—you who seek God." It does not say "you who *find* God." Why? True seekers never want to find God, they want to feel that they are always finding God, and there is always more to find and always more to do. The thirst for God can never be quenched, because it is an endless thirst for the Endless One. And indeed, there is so much joy in the anticipation of getting forever closer and closer to our Endless Self.

Notes

Introduction

1. Lev. 44:11.

Chapter 1

1. Talmud, Sanhedrin 65b.
2. Isa. 59:2.
3. From Stuart Hample and Eric Marshall, *Children's Letters to God* (New York: Workman Publishing Co., 1991).
4. Talmud, Brachot 63b.
5. Talmud, Sanhedrin 72.

Chapter 2

1. Eccles. 9:4.
2. Ezek. 1:1.
3. Gen. 12:1–2.
4. Mark Twain, "Concerning the Jews," *Harper's* (September 1897).

Chapter 3

1. Gen. 14:13.

2. Gen. 23:4.
3. Deut. 33:26.
4. Isa. 2:11.
5. Zohar 1:144b.
6. Exod. 2:13–14.
7. Exod. 2:21.
8. Ps. 130:1.
9. Is. 63:9.
10. Ps. 91:15.
11. Ps. 23:4.
12. Talmud, Chagiga 15b.
13. Ps. 27:10.
14. Ps. 139:8.

Chapter 4

1. Gen. 1:26–27.
2. Gen. 2:7–8, 15.
3. Joseph B. Soloveitchik, *The Lonely Man of Faith* (New York: Doubleday, 1965), p. 9.
4. Ps. 8:6.
5. Rabbi Soloveitchik describes Adam 2 in this way: "His existential 'I' experience is interwoven in the awareness

of communing with the
Great Self."
6. Ps. 130:1.

Chapter 5

1. Gen. 1:27.
2. Gen. 2:21–24.

Chapter 6

1. Deut. 6:5.
2. Gen. 33:20.
3. Talmud, Megillah 18a.
4. Talmud, Baba Batra 75b.

Chapter 7

1. Eccles. 1:1.
2. Pirkei Avot 1:3.
3. Gen. 25:29–34.
4. Eccles. 1:2–3.
5. Eccles. 12:13.

Chapter 8

1. Gen. 23:1.
2. Talmud, Tamid 32a.
3. Deut. 4:39.
4. Prov. 3:6.
5. Pirkei Avot 4:17.

Chapter 9

1. Gen. 24:1, 27:33, 33:11.
2. Gen. 33:9–11.
3. Abraham Isaac Kook, *Orot HaKadosh*, vol. 3 (Jerusalem: Mossad Harav Kook, 1981), 3:76.
4. This is the secret of the miraculous survival of the Jewish people, a people whose primary goal—indeed their reason for being—is to channel divine blessings to the world, to be a "light unto the nations" (Isa. 42:6).
5. Pirkei Avot 2:4.
6. Kook, *Orot HaKadosh*, 3:46.
7. Kook, *Orot HaKadosh*, 3:50.
8. Lev. 44:11.
9. Gen. 41:38.
10. Deut. 4:4.

Chapter 10

1. Eccles. 1:18.
2. Ps. 42:2.
3. Ps. 105:3.
4. Ps. 126:2.
5. Ps. 104:34.
6. Ps. 92:5.
7. Ps. 33:21.
8. Ps. 104:34.

Invitation to the Reader

Dear Reader,
Please feel free to write me. It would be an honor and a pleasure to receive your comments and questions.

All the best,

David Aaron
c/o Isralight
25 Misgav Ladach
Old City, Jerusalem
97500
Israel

E-mail: david.aaron@isralight.org

For more information about Isralight seminars and retreats, and articles by Rabbi David Aaron, see www.isralight.org and www.rabbidavid aaron.com.

About the Author

Rabbi David Aaron (www.rabbidavidaaron.com) is a visionary and spiritual educator. He is the founder and dean of Isralight (www .Isralight.org), an international organization dedicated to inspiring a renaissance in spiritual life, with programs in Jerusalem, Tel Aviv, New York, Los Angeles, and South Africa.

Rabbi Aaron has authored several books including *Endless Light, Seeing God, The Secret Life of God, Inviting God In,* and *Living a Joyous Life.* His books have attracted national media attention including *Larry King Live* and *E! Entertainment.* He lives in Jerusalem with his wife, Chana, seven children, and six grandchildren.